THE MESSENGER IS THE MESSAGE

The Messenger *is* The Message

How to Mobilize Customers and Unleash the Power of Advocate Marketing

MARK ORGAN

FOUNDER AND CEO OF INFLUITIVE,

& DEENA ZENYK

FOREWORD BY GEOFFREY MOORE

LIONCREST
PUBLISHING

THE MESSENGER IS THE MESSAGE

*How to Mobilize Customers and Unleash
the Power of Advocate Marketing*

ISBN   978-1-61961-842-8 *Hardcover*

         978-1-61961-736-0 *Paperback*

         978-1-61961-737-7 *Ebook*

Contents

———

Foreword

BY GEOFFREY MOORE

———

The medium is the message.

So wrote Marshall McLuhan in his seminal marketing work, *Understanding Media: The Extensions of Man.* In the decades since it publication in 1964, countless business and marketing students and professionals have read McLuhan's work, and have repeated and referenced that quintessential line.

Why, then, has it been updated for the title of this book?

The answer is simple: in today's socially interconnected world, the medium is now the *messenger*, not the message.

None of our traditional marketing and communications strategies were designed for the reality of our increasingly digital world. While the world has been living in the digital age for decades, we're now living in a new shift toward vastly greater social connectedness, which will drive huge changes in the way businesses interact with customers.

Digital marketing is immediate, fluid, social, and self-amplifying. It matters tremendously how fast you respond to a communications opportunity or issue, how adaptable you are to the spin the world will put on what you have said, how good you are at listening and responding to the social networks you are engaging with, and how alert you are to the potential for rapid escalation at any point in the dialog. How well you react to these factors is the primary driver of the trust your customers have in your company.

Your best strategy is simple: *be yourself.* Be authentic. Be transparent. Why? Because when the apparent you and the real you are the same, people learn to trust you. It is trust—brand trust—that is at the core of effectiveness in the digital world. Just as a face-to-face connection, a handshake to seal a deal, has always been more effective in the real world, authenticity in the digital space is crucial to how your customers will connect with your company.

How to do this, how to *be* this, is the subject of this book. The future of marketing lies in the enlistment of advocates.

We are in the midst of a dramatic reversal of power. In industry after industry, for the first time in my life, supply exceeds demand, often dramatically. None of our systems were designed for this eventuality. Demand has always exceeded supply. Product was king. That is why customers would wait in line; that is why they would buy whatever was on the shelf, whatever they could afford.

Today, that is not the case. When supply exceeds demand, the customer becomes the scarce ingredient in the economic equation. And in a world where the customer is king, vendors need to become more skilled as courtiers; they need to invest as much capital in relationships as they do in product. That is what the future of marketing is all about: building, nurturing, and leveraging true connections with customers.

This book will show you how to enter the forefront of this new marketing landscape. It will show you how to succeed in a world where the rules of customer engagement have shifted. How can you engage and enlist customers in a way that drives exponential growth, both online and in person? Read and learn.

GEOFFREY A. MOORE

AUTHOR, *CROSSING THE CHASM, ZONE TO WIN*

Introduction

———

In today's sea of beautifully designed, reasonably safe, and technologically advanced automobiles, one car company stands out in a class all its own: Tesla. This company has captured the imagination of critics and customers alike with an entirely new category of car. The three models that comprise the Tesla lineup are instantly recognizable, and represent to most consumers the ultimate status symbol. Driving a Tesla is like owning a piece of the future.

The appeal of the electric car is not a new concept to most consumers, nor is it a tough sell; after all, electric cars create a cleaner, more environmentally friendly mode of transportation, and remove the need to ever again dig out your wallet at the gas station. There had been incarnations of the electric car on the road and in the showroom for years—decades, even—before Tesla came along. So why, then, was the Tesla Model S such a game changer? Why, in March of 2016, did enthusiastic consumers wait hours in line at Tesla stores to put down a $1,000 pre-order deposit on the Tesla Model 3, a car that wouldn't even be unveiled for two more years? How did Tesla achieve such a rapid and dense saturation of not only consumer awareness, but the global consumer imagination?

A short CGI film titled "Fireflies" points to the answer. In October of 2015, director Sam O'Hare released a beautiful vision of the electric car revolution, a dance of fireflies buzzing with sparks that eventually coalesce into a shiny Tesla Model S. The car's recessed door handles extend smoothly, like magic, before its headlights brighten and it zips away into the sunset. The film suggests a future world in which gas stations and fossil fuels are a thing of the past, and allows the viewer to imagine themselves a part of that future. It's captivating, pure and simple. A company couldn't hope for a better advertisement of its product.

How much did Tesla spend on it? Zero.

O'Hare released the film through the production company Parachute, with the simple tagline, "...created as an homage to a brand we admire." He spent a year and a half writing and producing "Fireflies" entirely on his own, motivated by nothing more than inspiration and enthusiasm for Tesla's vision of a future without human dependency on oil.

People who watch "Fireflies" are struck by the novel beauty and excitement captured on screen. When they learn that film was made purely out of love for the brand, they see the value of the Tesla product line in a whole new light. It's the ultimate validation of the company's brand, and Tesla didn't pay a dime for it.

TRUST EARNS ATTENTION

The most valuable commodity of this century is undivided attention, and it's because undivided attention is increasingly scarce in the digital age. There have never been more distractions available, electronic and otherwise, wreaking havoc on our brains, which are wired for novelty. Yet the way most companies go about grabbing their share of attention from their buyers is outdated, ineffective, and, at worst, actively destroys their brand value.

Consider the sheer volume of sales messages that floods the inbox of the typical consumer every single day. How can anyone be expected to wade through the deluge of demands for their attention? Why, then, is this the method the vast majority of companies rely on to develop relationships with their buyers?

Most companies neglect to target the single most important motivator of consumer attention: *trust*.

Buyers trust what they know. When they don't know enough, they bridge the gap by turning to the knowledge of other people—specifically, other buyers they themselves trust. These trusted cohorts provide the best advocacy a company can ask for: the firsthand experience of the company's quality.

Consider your most recent major purchase. By *major*, we mean an item expensive and important enough that the purchase required research, perhaps a little comparison-shopping, and certainly consultation of others' opinions. What ultimately convinced you to buy? Were you influenced by an ad you saw in a magazine, or one that flashed across your computer screen? Did you receive an email from a company selling the product that had just the right persuasive language? Maybe you compared expert reviews and browsed industry blogs to learn everything you could about all the options. In the end, however, what piece of the puzzle convinced you which product was worth your money?

If you're anything like most consumers, that final puzzle piece was a simple conversation with a friend. Rarely do advertising campaigns or expert opinions have the same impact as the word of our peers. A stranger's obvious efforts to sway us, especially when that stranger stands to benefit from the interaction, builds little in the way of trust and attention. But when our friends talk, we listen.

This is the key to Tesla's massive success in brand awareness. Owning a Tesla is special, and owners want to share how special they feel. After customers buy a Tesla, they drive away in a computer on wheels, which is automatically updated every eight weeks, just like their phones; new features appear every couple of months, making the purchase feel novel all over again. Tesla makes its customers feel like they're part of something larger than themselves: a shift toward energy independence, and a celebration of human innovation.

By surprising and delighting their users, Tesla generates buzz without advertising or marketing. The majority of its customers—people who are willing to sleep in tents to hold their spot in line for a pre-order—are referred by other owners. In other words, they're referred by *advocates.*

Tesla builds its advocate program right into its cars. Turn the key, and an app launches on the dashboard that accesses the owner's address book and encourages them to refer a friend. If that referral signs, they get a $1,000 discount, and so does the owner. If they refer ten buyers, they earn the right to purchase a Founders Edition of the Model S with every possible option—a configuration not available to the general public.

Owning a Tesla is like owning a social-capital generator. People want to talk about the car, and in telling them about it, Tesla owners do more for the company's sales than any ad in print, on television, or on the internet.

HARNESSING OPPORTUNITY

The network of peers surrounding any client or customer is a company's best hope of gaining that customer's attention. Few companies, though, take advantage of this wide-open, and wholly undervalued, opportunity. Any company that *does* place its focus on leveraging the trust inherent between peers can expect brand growth that will place it far ahead of its competitors in the market. They will have harnessed the opportunity of *advocate marketing.*

Advocate marketing is the process of discovering, nurturing, and mobilizing a company's most enthusiastic customers to create a marketing engine that powers sales. Put simply, it's a system for making customers happy, and then capitalizing on that happiness to benefit your business.

Buyers crave authenticity. They want to trust companies

they can believe in. It's why review platforms like Yelp, TripAdvisor, and Glassdoor see so much traffic; peer review is persuasive and powerful. Advocacy, though, extends far beyond simple reviews and testimonials. Advocate marketing operates on the principle that, instead of leaving customer reviews to chance, a company can drive its marketing engine by implementing a central, organized, integrated system to generate significantly more advocate activity. By providing an incredible experience for the advocate, a company's brand engagement and productivity can be boosted to a much higher level. This translates into more consumer attention, more brand awareness, and higher sales.

Advocates are looking for something more than the simple transactional relationship of the customer. Advocates commit their time and reputation to a company, and they expect a return on that commitment. By compensating them with recognition and reward, they're made to feel special, part of a larger movement. They're not just a customer; they're a valued member of a team.

Few companies today do a good job of harnessing this crucial enthusiasm. Sure, most companies leverage reviews and testimonials to signal word of mouth to potential new customers. But how many companies can you think of that make their customers an integral part of the team? How many organizations build in their customers a sense of identity and purpose?

HOPE AND CHANGE

In 2008, a one-term senator from Illinois with a tiny war chest and even less establishment support achieved something that had never been seen before: he leveraged the power of advocacy and the deep emotional connection of teamwork to win the Presidency of the United States.

Barack Obama had been vaulted into the national spotlight after delivering the keynote address at the Democratic National Convention in 2004. While the speech was, as described by the New York Times, "a touchstone of national unity and a soaring manifesto of hope that would form the foundation of his 2008 presidential campaign," Obama's name recognition in the three years that followed wasn't anywhere near that of the other nominee frontrunners. Rather, it was his grassroots super-advocacy campaign that put him in the game.

We spoke with Obama's advance man, Rick Siger, who ran events, publicity, and security for Obama from the earliest days of his campaign. According to Siger, he was not the one who initiated the grassroots strategy; it was Obama himself.

Obama was not a dealmaker or a power broker. He was a community organizer who knew what it took to rally people around a cause and keep them motivated. He understood deeply what it meant for people to be part of a mission, part of a team. Volunteers who came flocking to help out with his campaign hadn't learned about him from a television ad campaign, a super PAC, or a pamphlet; they'd been told about Obama by friends, teachers, parents, colleagues. Advocates.

Obama's campaign focused on its volunteers. Respect, empowerment, and inclusion were the values that drove the operation, and each volunteer was treated as if they could make the decisive difference in the election. Transparency was a core value. Volunteers had access to extraordinary amounts of data usually reserved for leadership. If a volunteer did well, they were quickly promoted. This was unprecedented in the world of political campaigns, where volunteers were only reliable for a few hours of calls or door-knocking, and were historically compensated with coffee and donuts.

When Obama appeared at a local event or town hall, he'd invite the person running that event to join him on stage. He'd say, "This is my go-to person in this county. Treat her with the same respect you treat me." He shone the beacon of celebrity away from himself and directly onto the faces of his volunteers, elevating them to a special status. The campaign was an advocate engine from the very beginning.

These advocates told everyone they knew about the senator from Illinois who represented hope and change. They motivated college kids and minority voters off the couch and into the voting booth; they knocked on doors and lit up social media. They created a movement.

That was ten years ago, but the techniques used in that campaign comprise a master class in advocate marketing, and have never been more relevant to today's business landscape. They're still hyper-relevant to politics as well: in 2017, Emmanuel Macron, a political upstart with no funding and no base, was elected President of France via a strategy aligned closely with Obama's 2008 playbook. In future years, the power of advocacy will become even more critical to harness for anyone looking to become a player on the world stage.

IN THIS BOOK

We're Mark Organ and Deena Zenyk, and in this book, we'll share our combined experience and passion for advocate marketing, demonstrate what advocate marketing can do for you and your company, and offer useful tools for implementation. Mark is the founder and CEO of Influitive, an advocate marketing platform creator helping companies grow more efficiently by discovering, nurturing, and mobilizing their customer advocates. Deena is a pioneering advocate marketer, and is the Principal Strategic Consultant and Head of the Advocacy Center of Excellence at Influitive.

In this book, you will learn about the most important discipline for success in this technological age of the social and mobile web, and the dawning age of machine learning: advocate marketing. You will learn how to discover, nurture, and mobilize advocates to be full participants in the creation and communication of value. You will learn about the evolution of advocate marketing—where it's been, and where it's going—and read stories from a variety of companies, from startups to global giants, who are winning their markets by leveraging these techniques. You will learn about the neuroscience behind advocate marketing to help you develop the most engaging experiences for advocates, which will directly drive business results. Finally, armed with the information in these pages, you will learn practical techniques that you can apply immediately to power your business and career forward.

A NOTE FROM MARK: MY JOURNEY TO ADVOCACY

The examples of Tesla and the Obama campaign illustrate something I started thinking about more than a decade ago when I was running Eloqua, a marketing software company that is now a part of Oracle.

Eloqua was a bootstrapped company for years, with minimal external capital, so it was vital to win customers quickly after ascertaining their need for our service. At the recommendation of a well-known venture capitalist, I went out into the field to understand how and why people bought my software. I learned that advocates were the main drivers of a speedy and satisfying buying process.

We launched numerous initiatives to try to launch an advocate marketing engine, but struggled to generate sustained advocacy for the company. While the referral campaigns and case studies we sourced helped temporarily, there were never enough. Whenever a prospect required a reference or two to close the sale, it was a hair-on-fire exercise to find the right ones in time.

All that changed when we decided to host an awards ceremony: the Markies. Named for the marketing professionals who would attend, the Markies celebrated the marketers themselves. We presented beautiful trophies to winners in different categories. People loved the experience, and we generated a deluge of unexpected advocacy from the event. People proactively asked me, "I believe in what you guys are doing. How can I help?"

That's when the light bulb came on for me. These people were so motivated by the experience they'd had that they were volunteering to go all out on our behalf. What was going on? To find out, I interviewed dozens of these super-advocates over the following months. From their responses, I began to see the framework that motivates people to increase their advocacy.

This framework was validated through other experiences in my life. For example, I learned to speak Mandarin Chinese using an innovative product for the mid-2000s, Chinese-Pod.com, which combined entertaining daily podcasts and a dedicated online community organized around each grammar concept covered in the podcasts. This package was so effective that I was able to have business meetings in China without an interpreter after just a few months of practice. At first, I advocated for this service a lot, but noticed that my advocacy waned as the value I derived from the experiences diminished.

Meanwhile, my daughter Skye, six years old at the time, was so inspired by a "wall of advocacy" at her favorite frozen yogurt shop that she once spent an entire afternoon creating her own Menchies art, which still appears on the wall of the shop several years later.

Through my experiences, I observed three fundamental elements of advocacy:

1. Exclusive tribe
2. Moving the meter
3. Social capital

Exclusive tribe refers to the value of belonging. Human beings like to feel that they belong to something greater than themselves. The more exclusive the club, the more powerful the sense of belonging. This is why people paint their faces at sporting events or buzz brand logos into their hair: they want to belong to a tribe.

Advocates want to be able to measure their impact, which I call *moving the meter*. They want to see that their contributions are making a difference. The positive feedback is contagious: once they see they can move the needle, advocates want to do even more.

Finally, advocates want to accumulate status, which I call *social capital*, after the effect first identified by the social psychologist Robert Cialdini. When celebrated *within* their community, people feel recognized. When the experience benefits them *outside* the community, people feel validated.

When you combine these three elements—belonging, meaningful contribution, and social capital—and also make it easy and fun for advocates to do what they already enjoy doing—advocating—you can accomplish transformative success for your company and your career.

THE MESSENGER IS THE MESSAGE

In any business, it's possible to create a sense of belonging, delight, and mission.

Consider SMART Technologies, makers of interactive whiteboards, where Deena once held the position of Senior Advocate Marketing Manager. If whiteboards aren't as exciting to you as electric cars, you're probably not one of SMART's most passionate group of advocates: teachers.

Every year, SMART holds a teachers' conference. It's the closest thing to a religious revival meeting in business we've ever seen. The company flies nearly one hundred teacher advocates to the week-long meeting to celebrate the good work they do; in return, SMART ensures the creation of lifelong advocates.

After the conference, back home, at dozens of meetings throughout the school year, teachers hold demonstrations for their fellow teachers and explain how they inspire their students using SMARTBoard interactive whiteboards. These teachers know the product inside and out. Other teachers trust them more than they trust outside salespeople. For the cost of flying, feeding, and celebrating these teachers as part of the annual summit, the company gets an incalculable return.

SMART's advocates *are* the company's sales team, and so much more. They write SMART's blogs, staff trade show booths, participate in company hackathons, and dream up product innovations alongside developers. There's almost no wall between advocates and the company itself. Advocates are at the heart of everything SMART does.

While most companies struggle to acquire new customers amid the noise of this modern connected age, companies like SMART have an unpaid army of advocates to efficiently help acquire enthusiastic new customers. Advocacy leaders in just about every segment are also the industry leaders in that segment. Their focus is on building advocates and mobilizing them, and they see that as a driver of growth, profits, market share, employee success, and other key performance benefits. We will profile several of these companies in this book, showcasing a spectrum ranging from global multinationals to small companies with fewer than twenty employees, both business-to-business and business-to-consumer.

The skills required to build the advocate programs and communities that drive these results are new for many marketers. They combine the creativity and organization that is common to great marketers, with a genuine love for customers and their experience that is so often seen in the customer success role. These modern customer marketers are rapidly developing their careers, with promotions and compensation raises as they drive fundamental and measurable value for their companies. Our hope is that you, the reader, will consider building your business and career around the principles of advocate marketing, and will prosper as a result.

When media theorist Marshall McLuhan said, "The medium is the message," he meant that the dominant media of the time says more about the nature of that society than the words carried in those media.[1] The medium of our time *is* the messenger: the ordinary person who is authentically enthusiastic about a company, brand, and product, driving transparency and trust. The *messenger* is the message.

---

1   *Understanding Media: The Extensions of Man*, 1964.

An Endless Soundtrack of Self-Serving Messages

The hills of northern Alberta, central to our home country of Canada, abound with huge, depressing holes in the frozen ground called *tar sands*. These bitumen mines contain crude oil, as well as the toxic waste byproducts of crude oil extraction. The tar sands cover a geographical area as large as a metropolis. Although light sweet crude was once readily accessible throughout the world, those locations have been tapped to depletion. To keep up with demand, oil companies now have to dig deep for the oil contained in the tar sands sludge. It is expensive to mine, provides dreadfully low yields, and the entire process is dangerous, both to people and to the environment.

Travel all the way east and just a bit south, to the coast of Newfoundland, and you'll find shipyards littered with advanced and environmentally destructive technology. Here, they will harvest what is left of the ocean's cod, once so abundant that they could be scooped out of the sea with little more than baskets. Now, after more than 100 million tons of the fish have been taken since early European explorers made it to Canadian shores, the fishery must be tightly regulated before it collapses.[2]

Ironically, many of those fishermen now work in Alberta's tar sands.

In the same way, modern businesses have strip-mined, extracted, and trawled the most valuable resources we have: people's time and attention. Once a seemingly endless resource, the attention of customers is now scarce, their time fragmented by hundreds of digital distractions a minute, and a daily onslaught of sales messaging that overflows their inboxes and overwhelms their spirit. Companies must spend exponentially more money than they used to in order to grab what little attention is left. That investment generates yields that are barely profitable, completely uneconomic, and worst, dwindling.

---

2 Bavington, Don. *Managed Annihilation: An Unnatural History of the Newfoundland Cod Collapse.*

In 2010, Microsoft-funded research declared humans to have an attention span of just twelve seconds. Five years later, they reprised their research. The Canadian researchers, in both cases, surveyed a segment of participants and studied the brain activity of a much smaller segment. In the second study, they were quoted as touting the human attention span now diminished by one-third—down to eight seconds. Put another way: Microsoft believes that people now have the attention span of a goldfish.[3]

Of course, this is only a single study, one that has been questioned since then, and perhaps not worth the worry of attention deficits. In fact, the clickbait headlines declaring humanity's lack of focus could well be just another flood of distractions themselves. Even so, it's hard to deny that the always-on distractions that flood our brains with hits of dopamine have had a clear impact on our daily lives. The average office worker receives more than 120 emails and checks their devices hundreds of times per day. Millennials and Generation Z digital natives don't know anything else.[4] In the release of the attention span study, Microsoft CEO Satya Nadella now-famously said, "The true scarce commodity of the near future will be human attention."

---

3   http://time.com/3858309/attention-spans-goldfish/

4   http://www.radicati.com/wp/wp-content/uploads/2015/02/Email-Statistics-Report-2015-2019-Executive-Summary.pdf

Nobel Laureate psychologist and information theorist Herbert Simon described the problem in 1971:[5]

> ...in an information-rich world, the wealth of information means a dearth of something else: a scarcity of whatever it is that information consumes. What information consumes is rather obvious: it consumes the attention of its recipients. Hence, a wealth of information creates a poverty of attention and a need to allocate that attention efficiently among the overabundance of information sources that might consume it.

Internet browsing statistics prove Simon's hypothesis:[6]

INTERNET BROWSING STATISTICS (TAKEN FROM 59,573 PAGE VIEWS)	
Percent of page views that last fewer than 4 seconds	17%
Percent of page views that lasted more than 10 minutes	4%
Percent of words read on web pages with 111 words or fewer	49%
Percent of words read on an average (593 words) web page	28%

How do humans deal with this problem of allocating scarce attention resources? They look for trusted sources of information in as *snackable* a form as possible. For instance, the

---

5   Simon, H. A. (1971) "Designing Organizations for an Information-Rich World" in: Martin Greenberger, Computers, *Communication, and the Public Interest, Baltimore.* MD: The Johns Hopkins Press. pp. 40–41.

6   Harald Weinreich, Hartmut Obendorf, Eelco Herder, and Matthias Mayer: "Not Quite the Average: An Empirical Study of Web Use," in the ACM Transactions on the Web, vol. 2, no. 1 (February 2008), article #5.

Associated Press requires its news articles to average about 400 words, not substantially more than the historically 140 characters (now 280 characters) allowed on Twitter. Consider yourself an outlier for having picked up this book (unless you're half-listening to the audiobook while doing something else, in which case, you're making our point for us).

Edelman, a global public relations consultancy, conducts an annual survey called the Trust Barometer. This survey is meant to measure the confidence people have in their institutions, and the ebb and flow of trust can be tracked through the years. In the 2017 edition, worldwide responses suggest a crisis of trust, as people became skeptical about nearly every institution. Government, NGOs, CEOs, company promotional efforts, celebrities, and especially the media have watched their credibility sink to previously unseen depths. People have even lost faith in experts; the report suggests that the most credible people by far can be described as *a person like yourself*, and are twice as likely to be trusted than the media or company representatives.[7]

What is happening? While marketing departments churn out an endless soundtrack of self-serving messages—which we call *selfie marketing*—people are turning to their own social circles to curate information they deem reliable.

---

7   https://www.edelman.com/global-results/

The extensive amount of peer information available at the touch of a button makes it much easier for people to connect with relevant, trusted sources—people like themselves, who share their situation, worldview, socioeconomic status, and so on.

Brands must now scramble to be heard, but how many more emails can your customers process? How much more content can they read? How much more can they care? Most importantly, how can you win their trust?

Building a community of trusted enthusiasts—*advocates*—has always been important to succeed in business, but never has it been more so. In addition to the fact that it's easier than ever for people to connect with their trusted peers in decision-making, it's also easier than ever for your message to get lost in the cacophony of the endless message soundtrack.

Being an advocacy leader wasn't a necessity a mere twenty years ago. Sales-driven software companies like Oracle and Computer Associates were at a distinct advantage, because customers lacked a variety of choices. These companies relied on their sales and marketing functions to quickly scale; they developed aggressive sales forces, held constant industry showcases, and spent big money on marketing. Eventually, their interim industry dominance enabled them to invest back in their own products.

That approach, however, doesn't work well today because of the near-total visibility of product and company information. The game changer we've discovered is simple: today's dominant companies start by delivering customer satisfaction, then rely on those satisfied customers to do much of the company's sales and marketing work.

HOW PEOPLE TODAY MAKE PURCHASING DECISIONS

What is the best way to deliver your message to a potential buyer?

Consider the following data:

- 84 percent of B2B decision makers begin their buying process with a referral.[8]
- Reliance on knowledgeable peer references has more than doubled in the past five years.
- 60 percent of tech B2B customers search for peer testimonials or reviews of a product.[9]
- 28 percent of B2B buyers share online vendor marketing content with more than 100 others.[10]

---

8 Trust Barometer

9 https://www.thinkwithgoogle.com/advertising-channels/search/evolving-path-of-todays-tech-b2b-customer/

10 https://www.cmocouncil.org/thought-leadership/reports/better-lead-yield-in-the-content-marketing-field

Humans have always wanted to make themselves heard, from ancient Roman orators in the Forum to revolutionary-minded Bostonians on their soapboxes.

The evolution of information exchange is inextricably tied to the evolution of technology. The printing press revolutionized the scale and speed of information exchange; five hundred years later, radio began to replace print as the information delivery vehicle of choice. Radio gave way to television, which gave way to the internet. With each shift, the public has not only received but *processed* the information in a dramatically new and different way. The medium *is* the message.

MESSAGE RECEIVED

Marshall McLuhan argued that the nature of the technology delivering a society's messages reveals more about the society than the message itself, and that therefore, it is critical to understand the means by which people receive messages. McLuhan was witness to the birth of the television age during the 1960s. He noticed that the commercials that aired on TV had an effect beyond the advertiser's overt message: they penetrated deeply into people's consciousness.

Television advertising is a *lean-back* medium. Viewers watching TV in the comfort and privacy of their homes don't need to lean in to learn about potential purchases; the image, message, and feeling of the advertisers' products are delivered to them in their living rooms, and they passively receive the ads while leaning back in their couches. A skillful TV advertiser takes advantage of this direct connection to the customer's psyche. Back in the 1960s, during the birth of the medium, fears arose around the closeness of this connection, and the seeming defenselessness of the viewer. Subliminal messaging became a well-mined trope in entertainment, a bogeyman to which anyone with a TV set at home was vulnerable. Films of the period, like *The Manchurian Candidate*, warned that people could be programmed against their will.

McLuhan argued that any technology will eventually be taken to its logical extreme. For decades, there were only three television channels to choose from. People demanded more choices; cable and satellite television were born, and there are now hundreds of channels, each vying for a piece of the viewer's attention. Furthermore, with the advent of the internet age, viewers' options are now practically infinite.

With the arrival of the internet, the delivery method for sales messaging—the medium—changed, ushering in an era of inbound sales and content marketing. Email newsletters established a connection with customers. Web sites offered education. Instead of simply broadcasting, like television, the internet encouraged interaction. Companies that jumped on that bandwagon early built trust with their customers, and became prolific and effective publishers.

If you take internet marketing to its logical extreme, however, what happens is that anybody can publish. Hundreds of millions of people can post on Facebook, Instagram, and Twitter, and publish their own blogs, articles, and books. Audiences react predictably to the bombardment of company-generated content by applying stringent filters.

Most people only want to receive information from a trusted source. The most trusted source, if the Trust Barometer is any indication, is *a person like me*. Given such a climate, advocate marketing is not only effective, it is *essential*. To reach people, you must first breach their filters and win their trust.

Marketers must learn to market proximally, rather than directly.

Every new technology has heralded a twenty- to thirty-year cycle of change, and failure to catch on early in the cycle risks obsolescence. Consider the Encyclopedia Britannica; at the advent of the computer age, the company first moved its databases to CD-ROMs, then later online. They attempted fee-based access, but by 2009, Encarta had been chased out of the market entirely by the free-access Wikipedia, and in 2012, print versions of the Encyclopedia Britannica were completely discontinued. Travel agencies suffered similar fates as discount travel websites skyrocketed to ubiquity. Such is the fate of any company that fails to heed the current change occurring in social networks.

By contrast, consider a company like Tesla, which has learned how to break through social filters to reach customers. Rather than prepare for the current revolution, we should be mobilizing for the next one. A few short years ago, commentators warned of a possible employment crisis as a result of robotics and artificial intelligence. While globalization was once the great job killer, it is now automation that poses a greater threat. Self-driving cars will put taxi and car-share drivers, delivery drivers, and long-distance truckers out of work. Many service-sector jobs will also be made obsolete by automation.

Jobs will be lost in the new economy, but previously unseen and now-essential roles will take their place. To predict the future, it's imperative to examine the technology that drives it.

TRUST AND TRANSPARENCY

Transparency is essential in encouraging your customers to trust you. Some companies use a trust URL that shows exactly what they are and how they are performing. Salesforce customers can visit the website http://trust.salesforce.com to see if their site is down or whether their product is working; this instills confidence, because Salesforce is willing to show off their inner workings to their customers and the world.

Public reviews also increase transparency, and therefore trust. It's essential to encourage stakeholders, customers, and employees to leave reviews for the public to see. Companies worried about bad reviews should know this: your customers will discover your flaws anyway, and it's better to get out in front of them than to sweep them under the rug. Transparency is a major differentiator between successful and unsuccessful companies.

Advocate marketing fundamentally differs from traditional marketing in that trusted intermediaries deliver the company's message, rather than the company itself. Traditional marketing targets prospects, then sends messages via television, email, or other advertising channels. Like traditional marketing, advocate marketing does at its core rely on segmentation, but its medium of information exchange is the customer's peers and their word of mouth.

Even a century ago, experts understood the effectiveness of word-of-mouth marketing—it isn't a new idea. What *is* new is the ability to orchestrate and manage the process, rather than trying to catch lightning in a bottle. Word of mouth can be just as programmatic as any other aspect of marketing.

According to The Incite Group, 91 percent of B2B buyers are influenced by word of mouth when making decisions.[11] Of course, this raises the question: if you start *managing* word of mouth, does it become less trustworthy? McLuhan believed it eventually would. He observed that marketers do anything and everything at their disposal if it has shown results. Consider the deluge in recent years of reality TV shows. Success breeds copycats.

Marketers will eventually ruin every party they're invited to, said McLuhan. In thirty years, the landscape will undoubt-edly shift again. Using McLuhan's theories, though, we can predict that people are likely to become more sensitive to the messenger. In accordance, there will likely emerge a new technology that will aid in assessing the reliability of the message.

---

11 http://www.usefulsocialmedia.com/brand-marketing/
how-social-media-amplifies-power-word-mouth

ADVOCATES FOR TRUST

"Exercise transparency—even during a crisis or when a mistake has made."

—BRITTNEY COLLIER, MARKETING COMMUNICATIONS
SPECIALIST, BILLTRUST

"Companies should show that they are invested in customer success, and all groups should be customer-centric, which also helps to build trust. Build relationships with customers through advocacy. When customers get to know individuals at the company on a deeper level, it will help instill more trust. Advocacy helps with trust, because **people trust people, not brands.**"

—JESSICA MITCHELL, CUSTOMER MARKETING MANAGER, HERO K12

We Are All Advocates

Each year, a thousand customer-obsessed business leaders converge for a three-day conference with one objective: to learn how to delight customers and turn advocacy into a sustainable competitive advantage. Advocamp is a global business gathering hosted by Influitive and focused on one transformational idea: that the future belongs to companies that develop and mobilize advocates as their primary goal.

At Advocamp, we ask business leaders two simple questions:

1. When was the last time you passionately advocated for something you bought, or a person you truly believed in?
2. Why did you do that?

We are all advocates. What drives you to appeal to someone

else to use the product you were using, or work with the person you enjoyed working with? It can simply be love of the product or person, but we love all sorts of products, all the time, without shouting our affection from the rooftops. We all work with colleagues we find exemplary, without going out of our way to recommend them constantly. What constitutes the special conditions of satisfaction and delight that causes us to reach out to a friend and say, "You *must* try this!"?

WHY PEOPLE ADVOCATE

In our experience, a particular set of conditions encourage advocacy.

First, and simply, people like being on teams. Psychologist Jonathan Haidt has written about *hive psychology*, and his work suggests that happiness is positively correlated with a sense of essentiality in a larger team, and how this could be a human evolutionary instinct. He writes:[12]

> (1) The most effective moral communities—from a well-being perspective—are those that offer occasional experiences in which self-consciousness is greatly reduced and one feels merged with or part of something greater than the self.

12   "Hive Psychology, Happiness & Public Policy" by J. Haidt, P. Seder & S. Kesebir

(2) The self can be an obstacle to happiness (given our inherent limitations as humans!), so people need to lose their selves occasionally by becoming part of an emergent social organism in order to reach the highest level of human flourishing.

When we assemble teams of like-minded people to collaborate with, our brains are able to reach a higher level of satisfaction and fulfillment than when we work alone. In a similar vein, Biologist E.O Wilson further elucidates the human instinct for team-building:[13]

Today, the social world of each modern human is not a single tribe but rather a system of interlocking tribes, among which it is often difficult to find a single compass. People savor the company of like-minded friends, and they yearn to be in one of the best—a combat Marine regiment, perhaps, an elite college, the executive committee of a company, a religious sect, a fraternity, a garden club—any collectivity that can be compared favorably with other, competing groups of the same category.

Exclusivity makes people feel special, and feeling special engenders advocacy. If you can make your customers feel special, included, *essential* to your shared mission, you have

---

13   http://www.newsweek.com/biologist-eo-wilson-why-humans-ants-need-tribe-64005

created a marketing channel more powerful than any ad or piece of content your company can internally create.

Second, people want to make a difference. Small companies benefit from this, because advocates can move the needle for them in a more impactful way than large companies can measure at the same scale. And, as follows, the more you can measure your advocates' impact, the more satisfied they will be—you've provided them with a reward for their work on behalf of their team, and further confirmation of their specialness and essentiality.

Third, people constantly seek to improve their lives, and one of the obvious ways they go about doing this is through acquiring assets. People buy nicer cars, houses, and clothes, and join elevated social and professional groups, in an attempt to improve their standing in their community. The most powerful asset they acquire, however, and the one with which we as advocate marketers are concerned, is *social capital.*

Social capital refers to the relational transactions of trust and reciprocity conducted within a community, for the good of that community. Put more simply, social capital describes the value created when information is shared throughout a group, and individuals using that information can achieve satisfaction that, without inclusion in that group, they otherwise could not. Social capital is the magic that happens when people rely on each other.

Building social capital can include everything from giving your out-of-town neighbor a call when they've left their garage door open, to recommending a trusted tutor for a colleague's child. Social capital improves a person's standing within their community and distinguishes them as a person to trust. In turn, this more deeply solidifies their inclusion in their community or tribe.

Can you think of a person in your community whose opinion you trust and rely on? Perhaps it's the friend who always knows the best restaurants to try, or the coworker whose fashion advice has never led you wrong. You *trust* those people, and by extension, you value those people's opinions more than others. Those people benefit from the value you find in them; they are essential and respected.

When your customers advocate for your business, they build their own social capital within their communities. The more valuable they can make themselves within their tribe, the more likely they are to continue—or expand—their advocacy. Tapping into the instinctive human impulse to build social capital is one of the most effective boosts a company can make to its marketing strategy.

Early advocate programs understood this formula. One iconic program was Microsoft's Most Valuable Professional (MVP) Program. This trailblazing program grew from online Microsoft support communities on Usenet and CompuServe, where the company discovered that a core group of customers were the most active in answering product queries from other customers. The MVP program was a way of engaging with these super-contributors and their extended technical community and building on their passion for Microsoft.

Microsoft invited this group of developers to special conferences and gave them company swag, like patches to put on their bags, signifying their inclusion in an elite club. MVPs were more likely to gain access to people and resources unavailable to ordinary employees. Not all Microsoft developers were eligible to become part of the MVP Program, hence the exclusivity.

These highly-regarded developers were solicited for feedback on ways to improve the company, implying that their opinions held special value. Put simply, the MVP Program leveraged social capital by making its team members feel special and essential. We interviewed one developer who explained the satisfaction he felt:

"In my regular work duties, I'm Clark Kent. As part of the MVP Program...I'm Superman."

ADVOCACY IN ACTION: BLACKBAUD

Blackbaud's Michael Beahm embodies everything a great advocate marketer should be. He says that advocacy must be a two-way street. It isn't just about getting references or referrals. It's about giving customers opportunities to engage with each other, boost their careers, and be rewarded for their advocacy.

When Blackbaud launched their advocacy program in 2014, their first big win was getting seventy-seven referrals for new business in just ten days. Many businesses would be willing to wait a whole year for seventy-seven high-value referrals.

So, how did they do it?

For one thing, Michael engaged 150 advocates immediately upon the launch of the program, and connected with people by using the same principles that drove Blackbaud's customer reference program. Most companies have some sort of customer reference program, whether it's integrated with a SaaS program or is just a basic spreadsheet database. What Michael realized was that when you have happy customers in these programs—customers so happy they want to give you a reference—they're probably willing to do a lot more. He wondered about what he could ask of those advocates, and what he could do to inspire them to continue growing the relationship.

He crafted a program that would both reach people in a meaningful way, and help him reach his targets. He didn't just hit it; he exceeded it by 30 percent. Not only were the first days of the program an amazing success, it resulted in a deal made from a referral that covered the entire cost of the advocacy program.

AUTHENTIC ADVOCACY

It's tempting to take shortcuts to advocacy. For example, it's never been easier to simply hire evangelists, people who are paid to talk up your product or service. You can pay celebrity endorsers to spread the gospel of your brand, or spend a fortune on a consulting firm that will talk you up, but that's never going to catalyze the true spirit of your advocates.

Authentic advocates are ordinary folks who have genuine passion for companies and their products. They engage new customers like no celebrity can. The challenge for the advocate marketer is organize and mobilize these advocates; absent the huge paychecks sent to celebrity endorsers, how does an advocate program truly inspire its advocates?

The skillset of an advocate marketer is unique. Traditionally, creative people were responsible for writing, designing, and editing, and more analytical types were responsible for designing campaigns, buying ad space, and working with marketing automation. The advocate marketer sits right between those two aspects of marketing.

The advocate marketer needs to be data-driven and analytical, able to interpret data and make accurate determinations on who should be invited into the advocate program. This means examining behavioral trends and understanding intuitively the right times to mobilize advocates. Simultaneously, the advocate marketer must be creative and possess a high level of emotional intelligence in order to create the frequent, special, passion-inspiring moments of delight and magic that fuel advocate devotion.

Put another way, the advocate marketer is both an artist and a scientist. They balance gut feelings and hard data, psychology and statistics, emotions and facts.

THE SIX HABITS OF HIGHLY SUCCESSFUL ADVOCATE MARKETERS

1. THEY ARE STRATEGIC.

While this may sound like a no-brainer, operating from a strategic rather than tactical position is not the norm. The best advocate marketers start with a vision and strategy statement that serves to guide the ensuing metrics and tactics. Their strategy is their compass. It is the source of truth for how, when, and where advocates intersect with their business, and how they engage them. A strong strategic foundation serves to guide the alignment between advocate activity and core business metrics.

2. THEY CREATE CALENDARS OF PROGRAM PLANS.

The Discover > Nurture > Mobilize (DNM) advocate marketing framework is a powerful model that lays out the optimal advocate journey. It sets out the order of interactions most likely to lead to intended outcomes. A calendar cadence of when to ask, when to delight, when to learn, and when to give allows for foresight—and hindsight—in the planning process, and results in improved workflow planning and more predictable resourcing.

3. THEY ARE ORGANIZED.

The most adept advocate marketers are highly efficient in how they execute their program plans. This is, after all, an organized approach to customer engagement. To be organized means getting ahead of the spin cycle of one-off requests for event speakers, testimonials, and case study subjects. It redirects the time and energy invested in chasing down a small stable of referenceable customers, to nurturing and developing relationships with a broader cross-section of clients who jump at the chance to share their experiences with your prospects. Saying your organization is customer centric is one thing; having customers fired up to help sell your products is next level.

4. THEY LINK PROGRAM BUDGET TO VALUE.

The most successful advocate marketers focus their energy on a specific metric or two each month, and design campaigns or events to hit that specific metric in a time-bound way. For example, a two-week campaign focused on driving product reviews across a number of popular review sites. The incentive for the advocate to provide two or three online reviews during that time frame might be the chance to win tickets to a popular sports event or a $500 gift card. At the end of the month, the marketer reports on the total number of reviews driven by the campaign with a total cost of $500. S/he makes a clear connection between budget and value.

Excellent advocate marketers then report monthly on the results of that campaign in the language of those they are reporting in to. While metrics like advocate engagement and challenge completions are a good barometer of community health, your CMO, VP of sales, and customer success executive will likely be more responsive to understanding your outcomes versus spend. Programs reported in terms of business results and how much it cost to achieve those metrics are more impactful. And, in turn, by consistently demonstrating how spend directly impacts specific results, it becomes easier to grow your budget and portfolio over time.

5. THEY FOCUS ON BUILDING RELATIONSHIPS, NOT SPREADSHEETS.

The most advanced advocate marketers run programs that

are so strategic, so well planned and organized, that they essentially run themselves. This frees up resources for more authentic one-on-one time between advocate marketers and advocates. They use effective tools and are embedded in targeted internal processes and platforms to ensure their mobilization efforts are as efficient as possible. This essentially frees their time to focus on what drives ongoing advocacy: relationship. They are advocate-first in both design and execution.

6. THEY CURATE DOWNTURNS IN ENGAGEMENT.

The most unique trait of highly successful advocate marketers is the ability to curate when, where, and how their advocates can contribute. Instead of approaching advocate marketing as an all-in, week in and week out venture, they instead plan for high and low periods of advocate activity. Curated downturns are periods of time when there is very little activity—by design. The week or two after a big campaign, for example, is common timing for a downturn or rest period.

This seesaw between high and low activity serves three purposes. First, they conserve their advocates' time and attention for the activities that matter most, such as campaigns. In doing so, advocates have a moment to step away without any fear of missing out.

Second, the advocate marketer has time built into their workflow to build out the next campaign or work on reporting.

And, third, this rhythm of opportunity > rest > opportunity allows these marketers to nurture relationships at an arm's length from their ROI activities, such as asking for reviews, referrals, or testimonials. They create intentional distance between *give* and *get*. The further the distance between give and get, the more authentic the experience is for the advocate, and the more powerful their advocacy becomes.

The very best advocates feel *valued*, not just valuable.

ADVOCATE MARKETERS IN ACTION

Where do advocate marketers come from?

Typically, they start out in some other area of the organization. They may have experience in product marketing, demand generation, or social marketing. You might use specialists for key areas, especially within a bigger company, but it usually works best to place one person in charge of the advocate program, and make it their primary mission to generate and build an amazing advocate experience.

At Influitive, we work with advocate marketers from across

the landscape of professional experience. They come from roles managing content, marketing, customer experience, and corporate strategy. One common thread we see that they all share is their belief in relationships, and their focus on building connections with people to achieve larger business goals.

Sarah Lamb is a Senior Strategy Analyst at ADP who pivoted to a role in her company's advocacy marketing program from a career in corporate strategy. "My role is not 100% advocate marketing, but I've known about our advocacy program for a couple of years, and have always been intrigued," she says. "I leveraged my communications background to move into the role, because I was looking to exert more creativity. But before I did, I built the skills that made me relevant to the role: industry insight, communication expertise, a deep understanding of the business, and the willingness to understand and support my clients."

Says Ray Lau, Customer Advocacy Marketing Manager at PowerDMS: "Advocate marketing is blue water in a marketing ocean of red."

The opportunities available to those looking for more connection and leadership are nearly limitless in the field of advocate marketing. Most companies haven't yet discovered the power of advocacy, and the chance to be at the forefront of building something new is a tempting call to action for many professionals.

Natalie Gullatt is the Content Manager at Oldcastle, Inc., and switched from social media marketing into advocate marketing because she saw just such an opportunity. "I'd seen how advocate marketing could work well at my previous company. I saw the huge brand implications and long-term revenue that resulted. I wanted to bring that advantage to Oldcastle to help it remain the market leader." She'd already built skills in her previous marketing roles that helped her transition: she had a focus on frequency and consistency of communication, and she had a creative view of marketing due to her work in the digital space. "It's hard to gain engagement, but once you have it, it's harder to *keep* engagement. A commitment to regular engagement is crucial, but more important is *creative* engagement."

Some advocate marketers have come to the field after a long career in the field that is possibly most closely reliant on customer relationships: entrepreneurship. Laura Olsen, the Senior Corporate Marketing Manager at DocuSign, was the owner of numerous bars and restaurants before her career shift. "I was working 16+ hour days, 7 days a week. While I truly loved what I was doing, I woke up one day and realized that 6 years had passed. I had missed key moments of the life that had been happening all around me: friends, babies, marriages. My awakening happened to coincide with two unsolicited offers for my last two restaurant spaces. It was a tough decision, but I decided to sell. When I thought about my next move, I realized that my favorite aspect of being an entrepreneur was my connection to my customers. Since I was working so much, I didn't have time for my friends, and my customers had become my community. I saw the tremendous value they had in making me successful, and I knew I wanted to find the next journey with relation to that kind of community."

Again, *people* are the common thread. Connection, shared purpose, teamwork, and relationships are what drive the satisfied advocate marketer. "You have to really love people and understand their value," Olsen says. "No matter who they are, no matter what role they play at their company, they are the ultimate VIP, and you should treat them as such. Genuine passion and empathy for all people are what drive me."

THE POWER OF ADVOCACY

The immediate value of an advocacy program is immense, and well-evidenced by the success of the companies we've worked with at Influitive. What follows are some examples of just such success within the business software industry at the small, mid-sized, and large business levels. These are profiles of real companies that have partnered with Influitive; for the purposes of this book, though, since we're about to share proprietary details about their advocate program investments and results, they've chosen to remain anonymous.

SMALL

SmallCo, a small B2B software company, was interested in building an advocacy program to encourage acts of advocacy for their software within their existing community of customers. They were particularly interested in creating high-quality reviews; they wanted to be the industry leader in positive reviews, as they knew the impact this would have on their sales.

They started by building a small customer community that they managed manually. They invited target participants, along with customers who had high NPS scores, into a self-managed program. Through spreadsheets and emails, they would request, recognize, encourage, and reward acts of advocacy. Once it was proven that their program had legs, they went searching for a software application that could help them scale it. This is what led them to purchase Influitive's AdvocateHub software.

Having a dedicated software application enabled them to

create a personalized relationship with a much larger group of people than had been possible with a manual program. Their hub is full of unique themed experiences that keep advocates coming back month after month to drive the results SmallCo looks for. They have approximately 700 advocates in their community, and expect to reach 1000 advocates in the coming year.

SmallCo focuses on educational content to drive product adoption for advocates. Advocates are able to engage with SmallCo's products and services in an interactive way; for example, when launching a new Android app, their AdvocateHub admin encouraged advocates to spread the news and have their companies download the app to win prizes.

SmallCo has derived value from direct referrals, but also significantly from the strong position in their industry they have obtained from the review activity of their advocates. They are now the leading reviewed product on G2 Crowd, a site for business software reviews. They have also seen their average deal size improve from advocate referrals; their company-wide average deal size was $3,500, and they now see opportunities as large as $50,000 through their advocacy efforts. They believe their advocates are their best tool for identifying targets.

ONGOING VALUE BREAKDOWN

- SmallCo has generated $454,000 of annual value from their advocacy program.
- Twenty-seven percent of this value has come directly from advocate referrals.
- Twenty percent came from cost savings; they were able to continue to scale their program without adding additional headcount.
- Seventeen percent has come from leads generated from reviews and being the review leader in their industry.
- The rest of the value comes from a mix of activities, including increased customer retention, increased revenue from advocates, and leads from other forms of user-generated content.

MID-SIZED

MidsizedCo started out as a traditional payroll provider, but moved quickly into becoming a broad Human Capital Management (HCM) software firm. This shift isn't widely understood in their market, so they knew they needed to leverage the power of advocates to get their message out.

The head of their advocate program is a very smart, business-focused advocate. She has been with MidsizedCo for five years, most recently leading the market insight group. Based on her experiences with customer research, she sees the enormous value of tapping into an engaged advocate community for deriving insights from their customer base.

MidsizedCo takes advocacy best practices and executes them with extreme precision. They know their advocates incredibly well, and leverage this knowledge by developing targeted and meaningful educational content. They also monitor when their advocates want to engage with a content calendar that matches when their advocates—who are largely payroll practitioners—participate in their AdvocateHub.

To drive up visibility, they created a commercial that is featured on MidsizedCo's intranet site, created a direct link for business partner contacts to submit their challenge ideas and requirements, and created a closed-loop process by soliciting feedback following each interaction. They currently think of their program as *client advocacy*, and would like to see the program expand to a broader marketing advocacy initiative.

ONGOING VALUE BREAKDOWN

- In one year, MidsizedCo created over 6,000 client engagement opportunities, supporting six different business units. These engagements spanned sourcing excited clients for case studies, driving completion of analyst surveys, building focus groups, and promoting event registration.
- This methodology has strengthened MidsizedCo's client relationships by exposing them to unique experiences with the MidsizedCo Innovation Lab and Product Innovation Teams and their Learning and Performance Teams.
- The strategy also allows clients to provide insight and input into what MidsizedCo is going to do next, giving the company an excellent barometer to use when planning future strategy.
- Their current estimate for value derived from advocacy for MidsizedCo is $5.9 million annually, which translates to $2,952 per advocate per year.

LARGE

LargeCo had an interesting challenge before them in creating an advocacy program. Because of their indirect sales model, it is difficult for them to create and foster customer relationships with direct end users. As such, they tried a different tack: they created a community with the intent of identifying and leveraging the technical IT advocates within their customer base. They wanted to attract the technical influencers within their accounts, people who were often difficult to identify.

LargeCo's program is an example of advocacy executed well on an enterprise level. The administrator—the program champion and owner—employs a cross-functional advocacy team to help contribute to the development of the hub strategy and execution. Her team plans Advocate-Hub content strategy on a monthly basis. On the internal adoption side, she has worked hard to internalize the program within LargeCo and bring it to the attention of the company's global leaders.

LargeCo placed a strong focus on developing case studies and content. Without strong direct relationships with their customers, they needed to find other ways to engage them in storytelling. They leveraged their large company events to create special advocate areas that they used to sign people up for the advocacy program; they also produced specialized, personalized video invitations that were highly effective. Sixty percent of the people who viewed signed up as advocates.

When they began full-scale advocacy efforts, they saw a steady engagement rate of 61.5 percent at launch. Within a few months, this grew to 94 percent.

ONGOING VALUE BREAKDOWN

- Current estimate is $2.57 million of annual value created, at $6,196 per advocate per year.
- Twenty-three percent has come from leads created through user stories.
- Twenty percent has come from leads that are generated through advocates and closed much faster.
- Sixteen percent has come from new leads generated from existing advocates.

WHAT MAKES A GREAT ADVOCATE MARKETER?

Advocate marketers create opportunities for advocates. They're the internal air traffic controllers between the company and their advocates. They might ask for a review of a service for marketing, or an introduction to a key person in a new market for sales.

At the same time, they offer education to the advocates on behalf of the training and professional development department, along with a healthy dose of entertainment. The more entertaining the program, the bigger the results.

Advocate marketers spend a lot of time communicating directly with advocates, asking them about their families, talking to them about their vacations and hobbies. The advocate marketer is the frontline relationship builder. It's a very different scale from traditional marketing, which can address millions of customers at once; advocate marketers are concerned with the individual.

Advocate marketers also need to communicate with stakeholders inside their company. For instance, in conferring with the sales department, they might discover that sales doesn't have enough customer stories to work with. The advocate marketer can take that problem back to the advocates and gather the necessary material to fuel sales. Or, perhaps the head of public relations is frustrated because he can't land a newspaper spot for an important story; maybe the advocate marketer knows an advocate who has a connection. Say the head of customer service reports a complaint they don't know how to address; the advocate marketer can take that question to the advocates and source the answer.

Advocate marketers are expert nurturers. They combine their love of customers with creativity and organization. Event marketers, for example, make great advocate marketers. They understand that events must be special, but also know that it's the little touches and connections between people that create magic at the event.

Ideally, advocate marketing is a marriage of the human element with sophisticated automation. A great advocate marketer builds relationships with advocates and leverages those relationships to drive results, which come in the form of new referrals, leads, and an increased ability to convert those leads.

However, they begin, always, with people.

TURN YOUR CUSTOMERS' OPINIONS INTO ADVOCACY

"Work with the correct departments to effectively utilize responses from customers. The Customer Advocacy team should be working with PR to make sure testimonials are being properly used, reporting feature requests to the product team, and using customers for reference calls with prospects."

—SARAH BERGER, CUSTOMER EXPERIENCE
COORDINATOR, FORCEPOINT

"Customer-first businesses that create thriving communities have clear insight into what their customers think about their brand, how they're experiencing the products, and how they feel about the company."

—JENNIFER SKOGEN, CUSTOMER MARKETING
SPECIALIST, DREAMBOX LEARNING

"Show them the value of their opinions. What change did their opinions affect? Who listened? Who cared?"

—KAREN MOFFATT, GRAPHIC DESIGNER,
GENOLOGICS, AN ILLUMINA COMPANY

Modern Industry Leaders Lead in Advocacy

In late 2013, Carl Pei, an entrepreneur and smartphone enthusiast, was unhappy with the quality of Android mobile handsets. He had to settle for a product that was either cheap and Spartan, or expensive and barely adequate for his needs. He thought there should be a way to deliver both. He wanted to simultaneously create a movement, not just a company and product. Motivated by his slogan "Never settle," he founded OnePlus in Shenzhen, China, along with his co-founder Pete Lau. OnePlus is now one of the fastest-growing providers of mobile handsets in the world at scale.

How did Carl achieve so much success, in an infamously brutal competitive space, so quickly?

Most technical founders would have started by building prototypes and testing them with their target market. Carl took a different approach. His first product was not a piece of technology you could hold in your hand and play around with. Before building anything, he created the OnePlus online community, called OnePlus Forums, a community of people just like Carl: smartphone enthusiasts who didn't want to settle for second-best.

His community guided him in making difficult feature prioritization and design decisions—an innovative screen, for instance, an ambitious choice to use the Snapdragon 801 processor instead of the more common 800, and opting for a larger battery while retaining a slim profile.

The phone was created with the community, and it's no wonder that the OnePlus One was a hit. Carl viewed the product as the most important product of his bold marketing technique.

When we interviewed him, he told us, "No community will rally around a weak product." The core of his strategy was a strong product guided by community engagement.

What was even more remarkable was what happened after the OnePlus One was built and ready to market: this same community became OnePlus' distribution engine. In creating a movement, Carl drew inspiration from the rituals, festivals, and rites of religion. Instead of launching a marketing campaign, he offered his OnePlus One to the first 100 community members who destroyed their old phones and filmed the act on YouTube. They were the only people allowed to invite others to buy the product—and they were generally unavailable, leaving most people begging for invitations.

Originally designed as a prudent way to learn about market demand, these advocate-friendly tactics proved to be a brilliant promotional technique. One early customer sold his $250 phone for $6,750 on eBay in response to the frantic demand.

Carl now believes that in 2014, he likely had the highest ratio of sales volume to marketing spend in history: his $300 media budget produced $300 million in sales. The community members—who believed this was *their* product—insisted that their friends and peers buy the phone; they created promotional ideas and made it their mission to see both the product and company succeed. This was an advocate army that couldn't be stopped.

THE POWERFUL ECONOMICS OF CUSTOMER ADVOCACY

An increasing number of forward-thinking entrepreneurs are starting their companies in this *advocate-first* mode. Unencumbered by history or convention, they're better able to innovate in how they create and distribute their products.

What if you are running a large, well-established company in a highly-regulated industry with strong competition? Can a focus on advocate marketing help provide the edge needed to outcompete corporate giants?

That is what David Ossip has done with Ceridian, a multi-billion-dollar global payroll and human capital management (HCM) provider. Ceridian grew out of a company called Control Data Corporation, founded in Bloomington, Minnesota, in 1957. Before David took on the role of CEO at Ceridian, the company was a traditional bureau payroll services provider, competing against the likes of ADP and Ultimate Software. The transformation David has taken Ceridian through is a fascinating one.

To understand Ceridian as it is today—a high-growth technology company—you need to understand the Dayforce story, which starts with David Ossip. David was founder and CEO of Workbrain, which sold workforce management (WFM) solutions to enterprises with less than 100,000 employees. When David's non-compete agreement ended in 2009, he saw an opportunity build a WFM solution for companies with less than 50,000 employees using cloud technology. David raised about $30 million in seed money and recruited top talent from the Workbrain team to found a new company called Dayforce.

From the onset, Dayforce determined that they needed a payroll company for distribution. The Dayforce team targeted Ceridian and met the Ceridian team at the HR Tech Conference at the end of 2009. Dayforce had won Product of the Year and Ceridian was looking for a WFM partner. The two organizations formed an exceptionally successful partnership. On a target of 100 units, Ceridian sold 483. This proved that Ceridian's sales and implementation team could handle the product, and the partnership took off. Ceridian acquired Dayforce in 2012, and David took over as CEO of Ceridian shortly after.

What convinced the board that David should be in charge? His pitch on remaking the company was focused on three priorities: engaging employees, building great products, and delighting customers. Ceridian began prioritizing outstanding customer experiences, with the understanding that happy customers would be the best fuel for Ceridian's marketing machine. Ceridian placed the same emphasis on their employee experience, to help drive rapid growth with their recruiting machine.

The transformation was incredible.

More than 2,500 customers—with more than two million employees—are now live on the Dayforce platform, and Dayforce revenues have grown at a compound annual growth rate of more than 60 percent a year since 2012. Ceridian is now an employer of choice, with a Glassdoor rating of 4.3 and multiple awards for their engaged workplace and employee experience.

A central pillar of Ceridian's transformation in the market has been their XOXO program—an integrated customer success and advocacy community. Ceridian's XOXO brand permeates the industry. Recently, we ran into David at trade show and he was wearing an XOXO shirt. Looking around the trade show floor, I could see happy Ceridian customers sporting matching shirts. Ceridian's trade show booth had a special area dedicated to the XOXO program, where customers, prospects, and employees could enjoy conversation, networking, and the helpful guidance of Ceridian's customer success managers.

We call companies like OnePlus and Ceridian advocate-first companies. They focus their activities on delighting customers, creating advocates, and mobilizing them, because they know this is the quickest and most reliable way to become a category leader.

Industry after industry is being recreated by people who focus on delighting and mobilizing their customers. Look around, you'll see that the industry leaders in growth and profits are the advocacy leaders nearly every time: Apple in consumer electronics, Starbucks in coffee chains, Southwest Airlines in discount air travel, Tesla in electric cars.

In the software industry, where we at Influitive draw a significant number of clients, the old giants have learned their lesson. Companies like Oracle and Microsoft are returning to their glory days of the 1990s by focusing on mobilizing their raving fans in order to compete more effectively with advocacy leaders like Salesforce.com and Amazon Web Services.

The economics underpinning these transformations is compelling. Companies with a focus on advocacy are much more efficient than their peers because they have an unpaid army of highly effective salespeople and marketers. They are more effective, because they can better earn the trust of buyers, as we covered in Chapters 1 and 2. Their competitors, in contrast, pay huge sums for a division of marketing employees to do this work, without the benefit of the most valuable element of advocacy: trust between peers.

ADVOCACY CULTURE

There are three main reasons why customers have an especially high level of value to advocacy companies. The first is intuitive: these companies focus on delighting customers, and in turn, those customers tend to remain with the company longer and buy more.

The second is a little less intuitive: advocates also tend to be more resistant to disturbances in the customer experience. Because of the psychological principle of consistency, which we'll cover in Chapter 4, advocates tolerate a greater degree of product and service defects before abandoning those products and services.

The third is the most powerful: customers referred by an advocate and surrounded by *advocate love* are much more likely to advocate. They're part of an advocacy culture. Advocacy behaviors are encouraged and rewarded. As they advocate and help more customers get on board, their value increases dramatically.

The advocacy culture creates a powerful flywheel that can elevate a tiny company like OnePlus or an old company like Ceridian to industry-dominant positions at astonishing speed. Advocates beget more advocates. Powerful economics invite investment and recruiting of the most talented employees, who turn the flywheel faster and faster.

A moat around the business appears as the competition can't keep up.

Geoffrey Moore, the software marketing theorist most famous for his books *Crossing the Chasm* and *The Gorilla Game*—and the author of this book's Foreword—noticed these effects in the creation of modern-era software giants. He was so compelled by these effects that he created a new way to look at a company's competitiveness through the lens of growth efficiency. Rather than look at the departments of a company or its financial statements, his four-gear model uses the following four processes to analyze a company's growth engine:[14]

1. *Acquisition.* Build a relationship with a prospective customer.

2. *Engagement.* Create valuable experiences that permit monetization.

3. *Monetization.* Generate fair revenue in a way that does not degrade the experience.

4. *Enlistment.* Mobilize a set of customers to catalyze the creation of more customers.

---

14 Moore, Geoffrey. *Crossing the Chasm.*

According to Moore, these processes constitute the complete set of processes required to grow a company, and none are redundant. He depicts them as gears, because each one turns the next. When all the gears are turning quickly, growth engine is efficient.

Moore asks his readers, "Which is your slowest gear?" Applying effort to address that issue will yield the best results. For many companies, the slowest gear is that of enlistment, because there are people and processes tasked with the other three gears. Without organized processes for enlisting customer advocates to create more advocates, profitability suffers. The companies that perform best at enlistment have dedicated and coordinated processes for driving referrals, success stories, reviews, and other beneficial outcomes of advocacy, with metrics visible to top management and the board of directors.

LEVERAGING ADVOCATES

Advocacy can be a great equalizer, giving smaller companies an edge in the face of large competitor campaigns. In the age of advocacy, entire industries are being upended by new or smaller companies that focus on building and mobilizing advocates. Ecobee, a Toronto-based company with about forty employees, is an excellent example. Though they were founded in 2007, their flagship product—the Ecobee

Smart Home Thermostat—was launched in 2014. Since then, new releases and updates have kept their products compatible with nearly every platform in the Internet of Things, but they have not expanded beyond their single, original product: a thermostat. Nonetheless, as a small company with one basic offering, they are competitive against Fortune 500s such as Google, Honeywell, and Johnson Controls, and have won prestigious awards for their environmental services.

How is that possible?

They leveraged the power of advocates. Hundreds of Ecobee advocates took selfies with their devices and told personal stories about how the smart thermostat improved their lives. Each story focused on both the environmental impact and the high-technology aspect of the product. Through Influitive, Ecobee has amassed more than *seven thousand* brand advocates who have generated thousands of five-star reviews on Amazon, Best Buy, Apple, and other sites. Their product and customer-service processes were established and adjusted with advocates as their focus, and the advocates responded in kind.

Today, Ecobee has an active community of advocates who called themselves VIBees. Despite the direct competition of Nest—a company several times Ecobee's size—to the smart-thermometer shopper, Nest and Ecobee are surface-level equals. The number of five-star reviews is the same, and there is no indication that Ecobee is a smaller and relatively young company. Once a consumer looks deeper, they find that Ecobee's reviews are longer, richer, more emotional, and more persuasive. The genuine support of their advocates has made Ecobee the number-two player in their market globally, ahead of Johnson and Honeywell. And because they're the only smart thermostat sold in Apple stores, they'll likely soon surpass Nest as well.

EMPLOYEE ADVOCACY TURNS THE FLYWHEEL FASTER

Advocate-first companies do not achieve this designation solely through the will of the CEO. These companies implement an organization-wide imperative, with every employee participating. The best way to get employees fully behind the initiative is to make them advocates themselves.

Here are the ways Ecobee strategized to build its advocacy initiative:

- *Feature Friday.* Every Friday, advocates write a blog post about a different element of Ecobee's product. Advocates tell amazing stories about different features because the product is complex and there's a lot to discover.

- *Access behind the curtain.* When Ecobee launches a new product, they launch with their advocates first. Advocates learn about features before anyone else. Customers are invited to beta-test new features. The relationship establishes a higher level of trust and camaraderie.
- *Following the conversations.* Ecobee has a dialogue within their own community, but they also look at what's happening in other forums. People have questions in a variety of places online. It pays to go where those people are asking their questions.
- *Offline meetings.* While much conversation happens online, offline is critical. Every time someone on Ecobee's leadership team goes on a business trip, they reach out to their advocates and meet with them for drinks. They establish a relationship with them face to face.

Employee loyalty is connected with employee advocacy, which, in turn, is connected with customer loyalty and customer advocacy. In October of 2017, the Aberdeen group quantified this connection. They determined that companies with a formal employee engagement program saw a 91 percent increase in the amount a customer will spend over the lifetime of their relationship with the company. Before that, Aon Hewitt's 2011 survey of management styles throughout Europe showed that companies with high employee engagement had a 37 percent Net Promoter

Score—NPS, the score that Fortune 100 companies use to measure loyalty—versus a ten percent NPS for a control group. Companies with high employee loyalty and engagement were found to have more than twice the net income as companies that did not.[15]

BUILDING AN ADVOCATE-FOCUSED COMPANY

We could continue with hundreds of studies showing the clear links between employee and customer success, because business researchers are fascinated with these correlations. But we're more interested in making the numbers play out in practice.

Gone are the days when employees were happy to merely have a job; today, there's a war for talent. On Interstate 15 around Salt Lake City, billboards advertise for quota-crushing sales talent, and on the I-80 in the San Francisco Bay Area, they pitch software engineering talent more than the software that they create.

What's the best way to attract this talent?

Employees today are looking for an experience, just as they

15   European Manager Engagement Survey. 2011. Aon Hewitt. http://www.aon. com/human-capital-consulting/thought-leadership/talent_mgmt/survey-2011-european-engagement.jsp

do as customers. They don't want to spin their wheels; they want a calling. They want to make an impact, advance, learn, and earn.

High-advocacy companies tend to be great places to work. This is both a cause and an effect. In terms of the cause, it's a lot more fun to come to work when you have customers singing your praises and validating the work you do. It contributes to a sense of purpose, which research shows is crucial for employee satisfaction, particularly in the millennial generation. Since advocates shoulder part of the load, from conducting market research to convincing a prospective customer to sign on the dotted line, it frees up more time for employees to be creative. Innovation, belief in the core purpose, and meaningfully driving results creates deep employee engagement.

Smart management teams know that when employees are most engaged at work, they deliver an experience that creates more advocacy, as well. High-advocacy companies often deliberately embark on a strategy to maximize employee engagement by investing in world-class management practices, a deep sense of mission, and thoughtful perks. In my job as CEO of Influitive, I think of my employees as my primary customers. I know that if I can accelerate their careers and provide a great experience for them, they'll make it happen for the companies who pay us.

Forbes.com employee engagement expert Kevin Kruse writes:[16]

> Employee engagement is the *emotional commitment* an employee has to an organization and its goals.

Engaged employees advocate for the company that employs them, and this advocacy can be worth a fortune. By recruiting their talented friends, writing and sharing content about the company, and participating in culture-building activities, they help turn the advocacy flywheel even faster.

Looking at Moore's four-gear model, it's clear that an engaged employee base helps at every level: acquiring customers, providing the best experience, value for the money, and creating customer advocates. As valuable as this is, it represents a small fraction of advocacy's potential.

EMPLOYEE ADVOCACY CASE STUDY: MARKETO

Marketo provides an excellent example of how an advocacy program can pull together disparate customer-facing programs under one umbrella. When Marketo came to us at Influitive, they were already active in the advocacy space, and had launched a successful program for customers in

---

16 https://www.forbes.com/sites/kevinkruse/2012/06/22/
employee-engagement-what-and-why/#2b3814757f37

early 2015. The customer program they developed—Purple Select—focused on creating happy customers. Those happy customers, in turn, helped Marketo achieve some of their company-wide goals. However, they wanted to switch to an internal perspective, asking their employees to work together with management to continue to meet those goals well into the future. What they really needed was to meet employees' needs. They needed to make employees as happy as they had made their customers.

When Marketo came to us to work out the details of the new program, they came prepared, with several key targets identified. One was onboarding—how could they make the hiring process and entrance of new hires into the business as awesome, exciting, and valuable as possible for both the company and the new hire? Another was reputation. The final piece was education—Marketo knew that an educated workforce is a strong workforce, so they wanted to create a company-wide culture of learning and inspiration. They wanted to be more than just a place to work; they wanted to be a place where people would *want* to contribute. How could they open the doors of communication so that employee feedback wasn't just heard, but acted upon?

An employee program demands a clear understanding of what you want to achieve for your business, balanced by the incentives for employees. It's the same way we think about advocacy for customers: what's in it for us, and what's in it for them? In Marketo's case, the company would benefit from employees who felt acknowledged, inspired, and excited, and would, therefore, want to continue their time with the company. Again, just as with customers, the idea is to deliver valuable intrinsic and extrinsic motivators.

At Marketo, employees benefited from an interactive, action-oriented employee portal that created an environment for them to join in discussions. They connect with each other, as well as with leadership. Instead of an anonymous feedback form, which few employees fill out, employee feedback is now ongoing and ever-present. The relationship has become a two-way street.

An employee portal, even an innovative one like Marketo's, might not seem like a big deal, but 99 percent of all global employees are now members of the program, and each averages four visits per week. Employee energy and enthusiasm is on display in these numbers. Typically, a few real go-getters will participate, but in this case, support was widespread. Not every company can achieve that, let alone measure it, without embracing advocacy and the advocacy mindset.

PILLARS OF EMPLOYEE ADVOCACY

We directed Marketo to treat their employee advocacy program like a customer program rather than a conventional employee outreach or in-reach. Marketo had already come to the table with four solid operating principles, which they were able to turn into an employee advocacy program:

1. *Listen and Act.* The people at the perceived bottom of the organization should have an impact at the top. People in leadership roles should be visible and clearly relevant to all levels of employees.
2. *Develop and Retain.* Getting good employees is tough, and it's even tougher to keep them. Develop employees in their roles so they'll stay for the long haul.
3. *Educate and Enable.* Give people an ownership stake in the company and its success. An employee is more than just an individual contributor; they should be a member of a team with impact across the organization.
4. *Inspire and Connect.* An inspired workforce is made of up people who know that they're part of something bigger, and are invested in moving the organization forward.

All the pillars work in tandem with each other. As of this writing, Marketo's program is still in the early stages, but their effort had an immediate impact.

Consider how different a new culture like this can be for

employees who are used to feeling like a number. Once a year, HR asks them to sign off on company policies; maybe they receive a Christmas card from the CEO. Other than that, there's little interaction with the highest levels of the company on a daily basis. Marketo managed to change this entire tone by adopting an advocate mindset with their employees. They applied it to everyone, from the receptionist at the front desk to the CEO in the corner office.

THE DUAL FLYWHEEL MODEL

When the effects of customer and employee advocacy are combined, the results are tremendous. They form a system for sustainable growth and profit, an engine of success. It may be challenging at first to get it moving, but once the system is spinning, it gets easier.

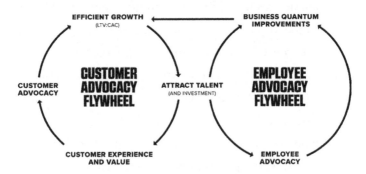

It doesn't end there. Many of the companies we work with also have a network of partners in their ecosystem. They're also customers seeking value and experience—when their expectations are exceeded, their advocacy can be more powerful than end-user or employee advocacy. They generate referral leads, share their stories of success, and often provide the most insightful feedback on how to improve the offering. International partners can help with localization of the product and more effective local marketing. Happy, advocating partners interact with customers and employees, turning the flywheel faster still.

HOW TO CREATE MORE ADVOCATES

At this point, you may be convinced that investing in your processes for driving advocacy is a good idea. Perhaps it could be the engine that drives your company's success and elevates your career. But what if you don't have a lot of advocates today? What does that mean for your company and product?

You may have gaps in the quality of your product or the engagement of your customer service staff. It's also possible that your offering doesn't naturally inspire people to talk about it.

There are numerous publications available on how to build better products, deliver quality service, and differentiate the messaging around an offering, so we won't enter into a detailed review here. That said, a core base of enthusiastic customers is required for the techniques covered in this book to work. There are some key principles we've seen that catalyze the creation of more advocates, and they're worth mentioning.

One common element we've seen with our most successful clients is that their advocates rally around the company as a cause. To paraphrase Simon Sinek in his renowned *Start with Why* TED talk and book, "People don't advocate for what you do, they advocate for why you do it." Carl Pei galvanized his OnePlus community with the *never settle* idea—they had a sense of entitlement to be the best. At Influitive, we have a client in the telecom business that has built a community around entrepreneurial freedom, and an accounting firm that's all about helping its clients become the *consigliere numero uno* to the CEO and board of directors. Having a cause that transcends the business is also an important driver in attracting the best talent, a key component of the dual advocacy flywheel model.

Another common element centers around the product. Advocacy is one area where product companies do enjoy an advantage over service companies. People rarely rave about their law firm at cocktail parties, but they'll gush over the latest gadget that has provided value and experience. Our advice to service companies who want to drive more advocacy is to *productize* their services and give them a personality.

The most important feature, in our experience, of products that drive advocacy is the removal of friction. Making something effortless that was formerly a hassle is a point of euphoria that gets people talking. Advocacy flows freely because the advocate feels they're doing the recipient a favor, and they gain social capital as a result.

While it's also valuable to have an experience that's low on errors, unless the alternatives are highly error-prone, this won't have the kind of effect that friction removal will drive. A high design aesthetic can also add value and experience to product usage; however, in our experience, a beautiful product in and of itself doesn't necessarily inspire a high degree of advocacy. A beautiful product that saves time, money, and headaches, on the other hand, is an advocacy winner.

Customer service is often discussed as an area of excellence that offers advocacy as a reward. From our experience, and from the data that we have reviewed over nearly a decade of business and hundreds of clients, customer service must truly be remarkable to inspire high levels of advocacy. Customers would generally rather not have to make a service call at all if they can help it, so decent service is table stakes.

What can move the meter is a *wow* moment, in which service goes far beyond expectations. Consider the story—famous, possibly apocryphal, but ubiquitous and powerful nonetheless—of Nordstrom refunding a tire they didn't sell. As the story goes, a customer walked into a Nordstrom store in Fairbanks, Alaska, lugging two snow tires. He'd purchased the tires at the auto parts store that had once occupied the space. He dropped the tires down on the Nordstrom counter and asked for a refund; the sales rep at the counter gave it to him, without a single question. This story has been repeated for decades throughout business classes, conferences, and keynote speeches. Officials within Nordstrom seem to be split as to whether or not the story is true. It doesn't matter if it's true or not; it's a *wow* moment, and that's what people remember and associate with Nordstrom as a brand.

We recommend mapping out the service experience to look for opportunities to go far above and beyond expectations, but at a reasonable cost. One idea we employ is to provide a personalized gift for our advocate marketing administrators based on our understanding of their interests. It doesn't have to be expensive, just thoughtful.

At Influitive, we benchmark our customer service excellence relative to *the best service experience I have ever had in my life*, which merits a 5/5 rating. If you want to have customer service drive advocacy, a rating of at least 4.7 on this scale is required. If you also have a remarkable product, you don't need to dazzle quite as much with your service.

ADVOCACY IN ACTION: MONGO

You don't need everyone to advocate for you, just the right people. MongoDB proved this with their advocate program for developers. Developers are generally thought of as introverted people, and research confirms this: a recent study showed that developers do, indeed, rank low in extroversion.

So, if developers tend to be quiet and inward focused, how can they also act as advocates? Turns out, they like to talk to other developers and are, in fact, passionate about connecting over their craft. Developer communities that appeal to this passion can be powerful, if they're plugged in. These people aren't interested in membership just to get a few gift cards; they're looking to be part of a strong community that offers education and networking opportunities. They want to continually improve their skills and connect with likeminded people.

MongoDB created the perfect community by offering educational content, networking, and recognition of advocates for their contributions to the business. They reached out to customers and asked them to tell their stories, encouraging a crowd not known for sharing their own stories. Through the nurturing within that program, MongoDB developed a crowd of advocates prepared and eager to create content for them.

The most enthusiastic developers became quite vocal advocates, who authored twenty-four blog posts within three weeks. They generated more than 220 online reviews on third-party sites, 500 social shares per quarter, 140,000 clicks on user-generated content, and 50,000 website visits in four months. MongoDB's brand awareness grew, and more developers started using their products.

When MongoDB set out to create a developer community, user-generated content wasn't at the top of their list. They were creating a networking and education community because they wanted to connect with the audience, but they discovered a huge opportunity once advocates were well-nurtured in an environment that felt safe, authentic, and valuable. So, when it came time to ask them to share their stories, they were eager.

Nurturing makes the ask for action easier and more satisfying for all parties. Customers need not dread a phone call from you, and you need not worry about them saying no. Instead, you offer self-serve advocacy. It's a choose-your-own-adventure story in which the advocate gets to decide what they'd like to contribute and what kind of rewards they value. Content writing, for instance, not only helps your company, but provides the advocate with exposure as a product expert.

In its best form, advocacy empowers customers in a way they've never been before. Now they can be a voice inside your business, with their byline on your blog, or featured on your website. Or they may choose to do none of the above, and simply contribute in the discussion groups.

Says Daniele Graziani, software architect and MongoDB advocate:

"These relationships keep me sharp, and when you're able to share mutually beneficial insights, you know you're a part of a strong community—one where you belong."

ADVOCATES CAN CREATE MORE ADVOCATES

If having an inspiring cause, a friction-removing product, and wow-moment service is important for creating advocates, how can advocates themselves participate in reaching those goals?

Every year, top executives go on retreats to rediscover their company's core purpose, their mission. While there's no doubt that these sessions can be valuable, we think more companies would benefit from asking their top advocates what *they* think the company's mission is.

One company we work with did just that.

Okta, a provider of single-sign-on technology, simply asked their advocates about the meaning that Okta played in their lives. The feedback was astonishing. One of their advocates said, "I need my morning Okta before I have my morning coffee," and he created a tongue-in-cheek advertisement concept based on a coffee ring and its likeness to Okta's logo. This message of essentialness and reliability became a rallying cry for Okta's customers and employees and changed the way they went to market. Now, many more prospective customers have resonated with the cause and joined the Okta O-Zone advocate community.

Customers may also be inspired to advocate when their lives have been made simpler by an intuitive product. Advocates also love to impart their wisdom and skills to improve products, and many will drop whatever they're doing to provide this critical feedback.

Security software provider CarbonBlack an example of innovation in this area. Companies in CarbonBlack's industry often suffer from challenges enlisting customers, as those customers tend to be risk-averse. Involvement with product design decisions, however, is fun and rewarding, which builds strong relationships with those advocates while gaining valuable insights. Recognizing this interest, CarbonBlack has a committee of advocates who review critical design decisions and participate in the creation of innovative features. The company isn't only saving millions of dollars on mostly ineffective focus groups, they're also building breakthrough new products significantly faster, and have a group of people who feel that the product is equally theirs. You can guess which advocates are the most active when it comes time to promote these new products in the marketplace.

Companies can also use their advocates to create wow moments in the service experience, like OnePlus has. The OnePlus 2 smartphone made a critical design error—ironically, one promoted by their community—to include NFC support. This feature was expensive, buggy, and generated a spike in service issues.

OnePlus' approach was to *hug its haters*, and invited users to town hall meetings not only to discuss their issues, but work on improving the service experience. OnePlus engineers detailed the current service experience and solicited ideas for *wow* moments that would provide surprise and delight. Service is now a strength for the young company, where it would typically take a company years to develop maturity in this function.

THRILL YOUR ADVOCATES

"Go above and beyond the call of duty for them. And gifts—they love gifts."
—CHRISTINE MOREE, SENIOR ADVOCACY MANAGER, BMC SOFTWARE

"Surprise them on their birthday. Write them a handwritten thank-you card. Such small and inexpensive actions go a long way, and help to personalize your company. They also show you have the time to take five minutes to show them you care."
—EMILY ELY, MEMBER MARKETING SPECIALIST, WEBPT

"Showcase them in customer videos, send them perks for things they aren't necessarily incentivized for, like social media shout-outs that aren't provoked by a company."
—LAURA OLSON, CORPORATE MARKETING MANAGER, DOCUSIGN

"For the tiny investment of some candy and thank-you notes, the payoff is priceless."
—BRITTANY LIU, SENIOR MANAGER, CUSTOMER MARKETING, HIRERIGHT

The Science of Advocate Motivation

If companies had to choose just one point of focus, customers would likely be the most popular pick. After all, without customers, there is no business. A company that chooses advocacy, however, actually increases their commitment to the customer in an indirect but powerful way. An advocate-first culture requires brands to develop a deeper understanding of the social and emotional reasons behind buyer choices. How does your company, brand, or product actually resonate with your market, and what do your customers need and enjoy? We find this by prioritizing the advocate, not just the buyer.

One of the foundational insights that led us to invest our

careers in advocate marketing is that customers seek different benefits when in their buyer versus advocate roles. When in buyer mode, a customer is generally looking to save time and increase their ability to make money. They want the product they bought to work, and they want service to be available if and when they need it. They are making a financial investment in your company or brand, and they are looking to generate financial results in excess of their investment. For users that have not bought the product they are using, they are investing time, and seek a return in terms of time saved.

When an advocate makes an investment of their time and reputation in your company, it is more of an emotional investment than a financial one. The returns are better understood in the realm of psychology than economics. Advocates associate their identity and ego with your company, and it is in those terms that they are seeking a return. While customers look for trust and transparency, advocates look for validation. As discussed earlier, advocates seek social capital with their peers, recognition of their choice to align with a certain company, and a sense of belonging to a tribe.

Even when advocates have been disappointed in a product or let down by a company, they may still be strong advocates. They can still be enamored of the idea behind a company and value their part in that exclusive tribe. Even if they're not completely satisfied, we have seen that they often still advocate. This is one of the reasons why we recommend that advocate marketing programs be driven from the marketing department as opposed to customer success or service—people focused on making customers happy can overestimate the effects of temporary dissatisfaction with a product.

Consider the actions Apple customers took when the company was foundering in the 1990s. When the voices around them started saying that Apple was going out, they became even more passionate about defending *their* company. The numbers looked bad—less than three percent of the computer market was with Apple at the time—but this tribe cared about design and innovation, elements at the core of Apple's mission. Advocate actions moved the meter, which made a difference.

What differentiates advocacy work from ordinary sales and marketing is that leaders work through proxies. In the traditional model, marketers target a prospect and send them a message, which is discreet and direct. Advocate marketing is different. The message isn't coming directly from the company; it's coming through trusted intermediaries.

Companies have always recognized the value of peer communication in sales and marketing. Company leaders have always known that recommendations from peers are more effective than advertisements. Yet peer communications have always felt a little bit out of reach, random, and hard to control. It doesn't have to be that way. It can be just as programmatic as anything else you do in marketing; it's just that the payload is delivered through a trusted third party.

Companies today need to build and mobilize advocates if they want to win. Mark had this realization as CEO of Eloqua. When he set out to raise a first round of financing, a high-flying venture capitalist named David Skok told him he needed to understand more about how and why people bought his software. David explained how he sold an entire year's worth of software in one day by mapping out the process by which people bought it. He even created a flowchart that recorded the feelings people had and the steps they took in making a risky purchasing decision.

The typical sales process at Eloqua at that time took about four months, but there were some people who came on board in about four days. What was going on with them? Using David's model, Mark saw that these success stories were a direct result of advocacy. The people sharing the success stories were folks referred by multiple people in a short period of time. They also saw themselves in the stories on Eloqua's website and identified with the people telling those stories. These potential customers were quick to ask for a reference.

Direct contact with references combined with on-target storytelling seemed like a formula for success. Mark realized he needed to implement an advocate-heavy purchasing process so the buyer would have no fear moving forward. That didn't seem so hard. After all, Eloqua had super-satisfied customers everywhere. They just needed to get more referrals, beef up their references, and put more stories on their website.

It turned out to be much more difficult than that. Eloqua rolled out referral programs, but saw only a small spike of referrals before the rate went right back to baseline. They sourced a couple more stories, but nothing was quite on target. Finding more references was even trickier; Mark and his team were pulling their hair out trying to get the right people to talk to prospects.

MEMBERSHIP REQUIRED

Some companies are skilled at creating a positive experience for their advocates. In the 2000s, Salesforce.com did so with a pioneering marketing initiative for their time, the City Tours, a traveling roadshow across dozens of cities. They went to various cities across North America and the world, inviting their customers and prospective customers to mix-and-mingle events. Everyone enjoyed champagne and hors d'oeuvres, and started talking to each other.

Surprisingly, even people who were not completely satisfied with their Salesforce experience responded positively to the parties. They felt like they were part of a club. People who went into the party feeling discouraged about the product or service turned around and advocated for the company. Salesforce knew the power of the exclusivity.

What would happen if you connected these people in a more focused way? What if you had a host or hostess who knew everyone in the room, and encouraged certain people to meet each other? What would happen if everyone was talking to the person most relevant to them? They would no doubt feel even more strongly that they belonged to an exclusive club and would want to reciprocate by advocating for the company.

When Mark first started talking this way, people were surprised by the focus on feelings. Mark and the team at Eloqua we were excited by these objections. Entrepreneurs love figuring out a secret—something nobody else knows but they know is true. Great inventors figure out what's unexpected but still true, and profit by going out on that limb and investing in it. The only way to figure out a secret, of course, is to diligently vet a hypothesis. Mark had done that, so he knew he was on to something.

THE MACRO-ADVOCATE MOTIVATION MODEL: PRINCIPLES FROM SOCIAL PSYCHOLOGY

Mark interviewed more than 1,000 super advocates—people who did more than 200 units of advocacy per year—to understand what motivated them. From this research, he created a model for their psychological motivation factors. The macro-advocate model steps away from the buying habits and assumptions that sellers make about their market to evaluate the target drivers behind loyalty and advocacy. On a psychological level, people want to be part of an exclusive tribe, they want to have a meaningful impact of some kind, and they—more than other forms of reward—want to gain social capital.

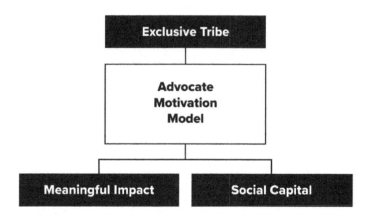

EXCLUSIVE TRIBE

What drives people to paint their faces at sporting events, or tattoo brand names onto their skin, as a surprising number of Harley-Davidson motorcycle owners do?

Humans have been tribal since the days of antiquity. In the very old days, being a member of the tribe was a matter of survival. Our sophisticated abilities to learn language, read, and influence people stem from our social nature. When a tribe has a feeling of specialness about it, the sense of belonging is powerful. Humans have a strong attraction to join these exclusive tribes.

The tribes that are most motivating are ones with a deep sense of purpose. Being a member of the Harley-Davidson Owners' Group tribe is much deeper than owning and riding a motorcycle. Encapsulated with their slogan, "Live to Ride, Ride to Live," this tribe is all about the freedom of the open road, an expression of personal freedom. Members of the tribe have their own rituals that tend to exclude the majority, including the tattoos, distinctive dress, and pack riding behavior. People buy Harley-Davidson motorcycles less because of their performance or value characteristics and more because of what the product represents.

Successful advocate programs tap into this primal need for people to belong to something much bigger than themselves. These communities have their own names and logos. The themes do not focus on the products, but what the products represent—the ideas behind the products. They are aspirational and inspirational.

At the same time, these programs are not open to everyone. People need to feel special being a part of the club, a distinctive status. Social and sporting clubs have long leveraged this principle to drive membership and engagement, and airlines use a system of levels to keep people striving to fly more. Many billions of dollars of products, from vacation real estate to perfume, use the language of exclusivity and status to sell more. It taps into a primal urge common among all humans: to be special.

MEANINGFUL IMPACT

Feedback is essential to the successful functioning of all systems. Even the simplest of organisms needs an ability to sense its environment and react to opportunities and threats. As organisms increase in complexity, success requires the ability to learn and adapt, which requires more frequent and often higher-quality feedback. At the complex design level of the human brain, we are able to learn rapidly and efficiently, with pleasure-providing neurochemicals reinforcing activities that produce desirable results. Usually, the brain rewards results that increase an ability to survive, thrive, and reproduce. Sometimes, reward functions can be triggered in less dire circumstances.

Successful advocate programs and communities incorporate frequent and high-quality feedback to spur more action. When people understand how their actions will move the meter for the exclusive tribes that they care about, they are more likely to do more of those activities. In my research, I found that small companies often generated a higher share of advocacy than larger ones. The reason provided is that the impact of advocacy was felt to be more significant for smaller companies and lesser-known brands. Well-designed advocate programs leverage this idea to make their programs addictively engaging.

Those advocates who receive precise and timely feedback on the impact of their advocacy are more likely to engage in more of that advocacy. A good program will provide feedback that a referral generated a qualified lead; a great program will provide richer feedback on why the lead was successful and the likelihood of becoming a customer. If the lead does become a customer, the impact of that new customer on the organization can really activate the advocate's sense of importance, a powerful reward mechanism for people. People don't just want feedback—they want to understand how they have moved the meter.

SOCIAL CAPITAL

The idea of social mobility is a powerful motivator for people to act. Communities naturally stratify, and people are driven to improve their standing in these communities. Animal communities often famously stratify as well, with competition over food and reproduction defining a hierarchy. When an individual's standing in the community is strongly linked to success in life, the drive to more frequently and effectively participate in community activities is strong.

The most effective advocate programs and communities provide tangible social capital for its participants; the best ones make that a feature of its exclusive tribe. In the early days of LinkedIn, circa 2003–2004, Mark was a power user of the network. He spent hours adding connections, and helping others make connections as well. He had a strong sense that he was building a valuable network that would serve him well in the future. Today, LinkedIn provides a powerful source of social capital for people, as a signal of their credentials, network, and knowledge—a signal of value that can spur social mobility. This drives an exponential increase in activity on the network.

Awards are an effective way to provide social capital for people. They are tangible proof of excellence and a signal that can drive career and life success. To generate more advocacy, provide your advocates with social capital—not just inside the community, but outside of it. Microsoft's groundbreaking MVP program did a great job of this. Members of the program would have access to programs and people not available to others, which helped them get ahead in their careers. They would have special badges to signal their status, jump the queue at events, and be recognized by senior company leaders.

The ideas of exclusive tribe, meaningful impact, and social capital are a mutually reinforcing system. Effective advocate programs drive a strong sense of purpose and specialness, provide high-quality feedback on the impact of advocacy activities, and deliver meaningful rewards to participants that improve their social standing. When done right, these programs take on a life of their own, and can make their brands shine brighter than the companies that have created them. The Ceridian XOXO program and the HOG (Harley Owners' Group) are examples of this. These communities in turn strengthen the brand of the parent by imbuing it with the power of genuine grassroots appreciation.

APPLYING THE PRINCIPLES OF PERSUASION TO ADVOCATE MARKETING PROGRAMS

SOCIAL PROOF

Burger or salad for lunch? You can't decide, so you ask your fellow diners what they're having, and they choose burgers. Well, that settles it—burger it is.

That's social proof in action. If you see a bunch of people doing something, you're more likely to do it than you otherwise would be. Social proof explains why product reviews are so powerful. If you're considering a product from two different vendors and see that one has a single review while the other has fifty, which one are you more likely to choose?

Psychologists have established the influence of the social proof effect by drawing on experiments you may be familiar with. The Asch Paradigm,[17] for example, demonstrates the power of social influence over people's spoken opinions. In these tests—developed in the 1940s, and still used today—researchers present a group of people with images of three lines, one clearly longer than the other two. They ask the group to identify the longest line. As obvious as it seems, someone will say that they're all the same size. The subjects will second-guess themselves and wonder if their eyes are deceiving them. The research suggests that subjects are just as likely to say that the lines are the same size as they are to say that one is longer, even though the truth of the matter is clear.

---

17   Asch, S. E. (1940). "Studies in the principles of judgments and attitudes: II. Determination of judgments by group and by ego standards." Journal of Social Psychology.

This makes sense given our history: our ancestors benefited from listening to the wisdom of the tribe. The human who decided to experiment by eating the bright red berries, or standing his ground in front of a wooly mammoth, probably didn't get the chance to make the same mistake twice. His folly added to the pool of tribal wisdom.

Advocate marketing relies on this principle. You might tell a participant that fifteen other people have completed a particular challenge, so they should consider it, too. It's likely that's all the incentive they need.

The science tells us that by pointing to what others are doing—particularly others who share similar characteristics to us—we increase our persuasiveness.

SOCIAL PROOF IN ACTION

- *Use testimonials to drive participation in your program.* Text and video testimonials highlighting the value of the experience can significantly increase participation. Both peers and influencer content work well here.
- *Make the participation visible.* Highlight the people who have already completed an advocacy challenge to *license* the advocacy behavior, make it normal and desirable.
- *Invite advocates to an online community.* The discussions in the community reinforce that advocating is a social norm.

RECIPROCITY

Ever notice when you step onto a car lot, a salesperson will offer you a piece of gum, chocolate, or candy? That micro-gift triggers a reaction in your subconscious. You're wired to give something back and relieve your obligation, slight as it may be.

Interestingly, the *give* need not be directly attached to the *take*. It could happen six months earlier. It's just part of the nurture cycle. It's fine if you give a $10 Starbucks gift card to someone and ask them to do a review. It gets an immediate result. If you increase the time between the gift and the request, though, you create a longer-term relationship. The amount of time you can put between the two events is a good hallmark of how healthy your advocate program is.

ADVOCACY IN ACTION: DEENA'S SMART MOMENT

Relationships are at the heart of advocacy, and they can be equally fulfilling for both parties. At SMART, I witnessed this firsthand while working with a Texas educator.

Rafranz Davis was interested in surfacing issues around the challenges minority students face in the educational system. It took us a while to get to know each other—Rafranz is not someone who trusts easily. She needs to feel that you're invested in the relationship before she'll plug in. When she did connect, I learned amazing things about her story, where her passions came from, how she was doing in her career, and what was going on in her personal life.

I gave her as many opportunities as possible to share her story, to give her a platform for her personal and professional development. She was excellent at her work in the school district, she had passion, but she didn't yet have a solid platform. Through a few different opportunities with SMART, whether it was networking, authoring content, or sharing her views with others, she started building a platform and getting noticed. Her Twitter followers grew from thousands to tens of thousands.

One day, after we'd been working together for years, Rafranz was presented with an incredible opportunity: she was asked to speak about minority student issues at President Barack Obama's White House.

It was the opportunity of a lifetime, but Rafranz admitted to me that she couldn't afford the trip. I was heartbroken because I'd seen how hard she'd worked to get to this point.

I told her, "Give me two hours." I scraped together the budget and approval to get Rafranz to Washington, D.C., put her in a nice hotel, and see that she was well taken care of throughout her time at the White House. Given my annual budget, it was a drop in the bucket for me. For her, it was a huge step in fulfilling her life's mission.

Today, Rafranz is in demand as a keynote speaker at TEDx, South by Southwest, and other high-profile venues. She's the Executive Director of Technology in a large school district. She's on the map when it comes to issues of education and color, and is a key voice on such matters.

This platform has little to do with her use of SMART products. The value is in the relationship. She helped us reach our goals, and we helped her reach hers.

Reciprocity is the *I scratch your back, you scratch mine* mentality, but you've got to be careful to correctly apply the principle. Too many quick hits encourage a highly transactional relationship, whereas a longer-term approach builds loyalty. Instead of offering a Starbucks gift card in return for a review, you might just offer a gift card on the person's birthday, no strings attached. Chances are, they'll remember this thoughtful gift when you do make a request in the future, and it will mean more because it's personal.

One study involved waiters giving mints to restaurant patrons when handing them their bill. Providing diners a single mint increased tips by about three percent. When two mints were given, tips nearly quintupled, up to 14 percent. But if the waiter outright acknowledged to the guests that he was giving them an extra mint, tips soared 23 percent.[18]

The key to using the principle of reciprocity is to be the first to give and to ensure that what you give is personalized and unexpected.

---

18 Sweetening the Till: The Use of Candy to Increase Restaurant
    Tipping. 2002. http://citeseerx.ist.psu.edu/viewdoc/
    download?doi=10.1.1.960.1118&rep=rep1&type=pdf

RECIPROCITY IN ACTION

- *Provide a small reward after the advocate engages with the program for the first time.* This is a little hit of dopamine that will spur further action. A gift card for a cup of coffee from Starbucks or a $5 donation to charity can work well here.
- *Provide larger rewards at random times, not just after completing advocacy tasks.* Psychologists have shown that gaining variable rewards and variable times have an addictive quality to them—this corresponds well to how slot machines work. While effective advocate programs also provide a clear path how to gain rewards, the best ones have a random quality to them, which drives more advocacy.
- *Provide special content only available for members.* A video recorded by your CEO or an exclusive e-book not only activates reciprocity, but also makes advocates feel like the VIPs they are.

IMAGE

When you're presented with an idea that appeals to your own internal self-image, you're more likely to convert to that idea. People have a need to feel consistent in the things they say and do, and by leveraging that and getting people to make small commitments and actions, they're more likely to make larger commitments later.

In a famous set of studies, researchers found that very few

people would be willing to erect an unsightly wooden board on their front lawn to support a drive-safely campaign in their neighborhood.

However, in a similar neighborhood close by, four times as many homeowners indicated that they would be willing to erect this unsightly billboard. Why? Because ten days previously, they had agreed to place a small postcard in the front window of their homes that signaled their support for the drive-safely campaign. That small card was the initial commitment that led to a 400 percent increase in a much bigger but still consistent change.

That's why, at Influitive, we don't make huge asks of people when they first start with an advocacy program. We start with a simple request, like their name, so they can follow us on Twitter. It only requires a single button click. When Influitive was just starting out, Mark simply asked people what their favorite color was. The micro-commitment of writing down their favorite color was enough to trigger the reciprocity principle and create a sense of obligation to act consistently with their prior action.

IMAGE IN ACTION

- *Brand the program according to the aspirations of the advocates.* Interview your advocates to find out why they appreciate your company and products, and what they aspire to be. One of our customers, a document management company that serves regulated industries and governments, found out that their advocates see themselves as warriors fighting against bureaucracy and inefficient paper-driven processes. They used this idea to brand their program and the advocacy challenges in them.
- *Gain small commitments in order to obtain larger ones later.* Like the foot-in-the-door technique from used car lots, gaining small commitments—like a follow on social media, watching a video, or providing feedback—paves the path to a larger commitment, like speaking on stage at your conference.

AUTHORITY

People follow the lead of credible, knowledgeable experts. The appearance of authority is powerful. We leverage this principle to some degree in our advocate programs by presenting an official look to all our content. Our programs carry the company logo, as well as a specific advocate program logo. The advocate program carries the approval of the top people in the company. Often, invitations to participate will come from someone in authority—the CEO or CMO—to increase the perceived importance of the invitation and the program. These logos and signatures convey our *imprimatur,* our signal that the invitation is of high value. Research tells us is that it's important to signal to others what makes you a credible, knowledgeable authority before you make your influence attempt.

Advocates value access to leaders. Some CEOs will record videos that advocates can access if they reach a certain level in the program, for instance. In-person contact is even better. Having advocate marketers and salespeople at events is useful, but the real magic happens when the president stops by to shake hands and offer thanks in person.

AUTHORITY IN ACTION

- *Make the program visually appealing.* Professional-looking design creates an air of authority and invites participation.
- *Use videos of your key leaders and senior advocates.* Videos of senior leaders both humanize the program and convey authority.
- *Provide opportunities for advocates to increase their authority.* These opportunities could include helping write blog posts and articles, or speaking on video and onstage.

LIKING

We're influenced by the things we like. This is a simple concept, but a powerful one nonetheless—Facebook, after all, has built a multi-billion-dollar business around it. Great salespeople and politicians are usually extremely likable, which makes them more effective. Advocates engage so much in a well-run advocate program because they like the person running it. They build a relationship with the program administrator. *Liking* is the number-one factor in the long-term success of advocate programs.

These relationships grow like any other. When you initially meet someone, you don't want to say or ask too much. The more comfortable you become over time, the less awkward such conversations become.

Persuasion science tells us that there are three important factors to liking. First, we like people who are similar to us; second, we like people who pay us compliments; and third, we like people who cooperate with us toward mutual goals.

The key is that the likability must be authentic. A manufactured persona won't work long-term. You can't be everything to everyone. Good advocate marketers are naturally curious about peoples' stories; they're genuinely interested in finding out what makes other people tick.

LIKING IN ACTION

- *Understand the advocates as people.* Maintain a record of advocates' work relationships, family members, and hobbies, and reference those in communications. Successful advocate programs have a personal quality to them.
- *Persuade like a human.* Stay away from formal speech and jargon-laden content. Just sound normal, with natural enthusiasm. Explain the impact that the advocacy will make on the business. For example, instead of asking for referrals, highlight the attractiveness of a new market and ask your advocates for help on breaking in.

SCARCITY

If you believe something is going to run out, you're more likely to buy it. People are hardwired to want things that are rare or scarce, because historically speaking, those things usually offer valuable survival and reproductive benefits.

British Airways announced in 2003 that they it had become too expensive to keep operating their twice-daily London-to-New York Concorde flight. The next day, sales skyrocketed. Nothing changed about the Concorde itself— it didn't fly any faster, the service didn't get any better, and the fare didn't drop. It simply became a scarcer resource, prompting people to want it more.

Some of the most effective advocate programs create scarcity through the use of a limited timeframe. At Influitive, we recently ran an internal referral contest with a deadline, and we smashed our previous record. We generated a year's worth of referral leads in a month. The limit can be subtler, like the dates put on company swag. SMART's advocate program did this with an annual backpack; when people came into the program, they got a computer backpack with the logo on it—nice, but no big deal. Each year, though, the backpack changed just a little. Over time, it became part of its owner's social status. If you see someone who has the same 2007 bag you're carrying, the two of you are part of an exclusive club.

The backpacks cost the company $20 per unit, but became a core driver of engagement in the program. It's the same concept used by Microsoft's MVP program: branded gear carries a high social status, because only people "in the know" understand its meaning.

If advocate programs like this work so well, why aren't *all* employees invited to join? Exclusivity is another form of scarcity, which is a crucial aspect of the program's draw. We ask people to apply to our advocate program, and caution them that not everybody gets in. We state upfront that we typically accept just 25 percent of applicants.

When it comes to effectively persuading others using the

principle of scarcity, it isn't enough simply to tell people about the benefits they'll gain if they choose your products and services. You also need to point out what is unique about your proposition and what they stand to lose if they fail to consider your proposal.

SCARCITY IN ACTION

- *Establish a timeline.* If it's the ability to participate on a webinar with prospects, for example, tell advocate users that signup closes Friday at noon.
- *Put a number on it.* Alternately, you can declare that your opportunity to interact with a journalist or blogger is capped at three, and two people have already accepted the invitation.

THE MICRO-ADVOCATE MOTIVATION MODEL: PRINCIPLES FROM THE BEHAVIORAL PSYCHOLOGY OF GAMING

Macro-motivation models appeal to the higher-order cognitive and emotional aspects that are unique to humans. Micro-motivation models, on the other hand, focus on a much more ancient aspect of our cognitive evolutionary history: reward.

With so many distractions and competing priorities, it can be difficult to get consistent engagement from advocates.

For example, customers have limited patience for learning how to use new digital applications, even those that promise a large return on the investment of time. This poses a challenge for advocate marketers who want to motivate advocates to increase their level and quality of activity through the use of digital platforms.

One class of applications that do not seem to have much trouble at all attracting users and engagement, however, is video games. Games have won the Darwinian struggle for what is becoming one of the most valuable commodities in the modern world: human attention. It is worth studying video game design to apply insights to the creation of effective advocate programs that are naturally engaging and drive action.

Researcher Dr. B.J. Fogg, founder and lead investigator for the Persuasive Technology Lab at Stanford University, has put forth an elegant theory as to what makes successful games so effective at engaging people, in some cases for years or even a lifetime of playing. According to Fogg, three elements must converge at the same moment for a behavior to occur: motivation, ability, and trigger.

Motivation primarily stems from emotions of pleasure/ pain, hope/fear, and social acceptance/rejection. Factors that drive ability include time, money, physical effort, brain cycles, social deviance, and non-routine. Triggers are cues, the spark that causes someone to pay attention. When there is sufficient motivation and ability, a trigger will cause a behavior to occur.[19]

The elegance of this model is in how motivation and ability can be leveraged against each other. When someone has a high motivation, they may be willing to invest a lot of time, money, and brain cycles, even without much ability. Similarly, with a high level of ability, the motivation required to complete a task is reduced. Since a core motivator is a feeling of self-importance and contribution—what Daniel Pink, another traveler in this thought-space, calls *the drive of mastery*—a skilled game designer ratchets up the difficulty level just enough as the player improves ability so that the game is always interesting.

Let's look at an example: no-limit Texas hold 'em poker. The World Series of Poker, the largest and richest poker tournament held every summer in Las Vegas, has legitimized a game notoriously associated with gangsters and outlaws of the Old West. It's now common to see clips of some memorable game-winning hands on the television at bars, and coverage of tournaments in the sports section of newspapers. The WSOP has recently created a fabulously-

---

19 https://141nho47iozd1l75s22eer06-wpengine.netdna-ssl.com/wp-content/
    uploads/2013/06/Fogg-Model-2.png

designed mobile game that is in many ways more engaging than the real-life version.

Mark is an avid player of the game. The core motivators for him in playing the game are a drive to improve his abilities to do rapid mental math, read people, and master his emotional state—all things that are important in his roles of company CEO and parent. The pleasure of making real or virtual money also plays a role. Since poker is a social game, improving skills provides additional opportunities to make valuable connections. These motivators keep Mark engaged to keep improving as his opponents get better and the stakes get higher.

Every successful game employs many of the same techniques. They build habits by appealing to core motivators, easing players through ability challenges, and employ triggers to keep people coming back. Successful digital applications use these techniques as well. Consider social media apps: they employ powerful triggers of relevant social information, the physical action of scrolling through feeds with golden nuggets of information (variable rewards), and the social investment made in building connections. It's no wonder that sports like golf and skiing are in steep decline in the face of screen-based competition, which requires dramatically lower motivation and ability levels while having more frequent and more powerful triggers for engagement.

The sophisticated game designer knows that people have different motivations for playing. Richard Bartle, a writer, professor, and researcher in the gamification field, has codified a taxonomic model for the different types of gamers and their motivators.

- *Killers* are motivated by competition; they enjoy the thrill of winning. Leaderboards appeal to them.
- *Achievers* are motivated by accomplishing goals and improving skills. Achievement badges appeal to them.
- *Socializers* are motivated by making new friends and developing deeper relationships. Social features appeal to them.
- *Explorers* are motivated by discoveries. Uncovering information about the inner workings of the game appeals to them.

While all people have a mix of these qualities, most people have a dominant leaning. In Mark's case, for example, he's primarily motivated by achievement. Depending on his mood, however, his other motivators can be strong. If he's having a bad day, the thought of thrashing the competition and winning all their chips is quite attractive.

We have learned through experience that advocates classify on some similar lines: competition, achievement, social development, and exploration. There is much in common between a well-designed advocate program and a well-designed game. Even advocate communities that do not have an online component, like a number of customer advisory boards we have studied, could benefit from the insights of game designers. Adding habit loops, and designing for the motivations of different types of advocates, can both multiply the number of advocates engaging and increase the quality and quantity of their engagement.

MOTIVATION OR MANIPULATION?

A final word here on the ethics of these techniques before we learn how to apply them in detail in the next chapter. These techniques are powerful; the macro- and micro-engagement models, when combined, can increase quality activity in an advocate community exponentially. However, there are critics who see these programs as a form of manipulation. It's a charge with some merit, and worth a discussion.

We live in the age of abundance. For the first time ever, the number of overweight people in the world is greater than the number of malnourished. Africa and South Asia have high smartphone penetration and increasing sophistication of products and services. When basic needs are covered, it's the superior *experience* that wins the battle for scarce attention; no more are survival resources the primary focus of the population.

To create an effective advocate program and community, it will pay off to design it in a way that provides the best possible experience for advocates. Putting the macro model of engagement, with its powerful sense of purpose, belonging, social capital, and feedback, together with the micro model that applies triggered habit loops and continual development of mastery, provides the most satisfying experience. We see this less as manipulation, and more as a removal of friction and an addition of joy that should be a part of any life or business endeavor.

In Mark's roles as CEO and parent, providing great experiences is at the top of his priorities. Yelling at employees and kids to do what they are told to do does not yield great results. Daniel Pink made a good case in his book *Drive* that people are motivated by the triangle of autonomy, mastery, and purpose. These factors are what a well-designed advocate program drives for its participants as well.

Manipulation implies that the company is the sole beneficiary of advocate activity, and that the advocate is being duped into doing things against their will and against their interests. However, if everyone benefits—especially the advocate—then it's simply a great experience, not manipulation. At the heart of successful advocate programs is fundamental and measurable value for the advocates.

It actually does not take a lot of work to get people to advocate for a worthy product, brand or company. After all, as we have explored, people naturally advocate. If you want to grow your advocate base beyond the truly hardcore raving fans with proverbial tattoos of your brand, and maximize your advocates' activity and productivity, then designing a program that removes as much friction and adds as much delight as possible will pay great dividends.

ENCOURAGE AN ADVOCATE-
FIRST ETHOS

"It has to start from the top: if customer-first is a priority with the Exec team, it will be a priority company-wide."

—MARGAUX, PRODUCT MARKETING MANAGER, VIRGIN PULSE

"Our advocates benefit in four key areas:

1. **Status:** The more they participate, the more they will be recognized as PowerDMS experts.

2. **Access:** PowerDMS Champions gain access to new features before we release them to our general customer base. Champions can also network with our higher-ups.

3. **Power:** We rely on feedback from our Champions when we improve PowerDMS. They have a direct say in making our product better.

4. **Stuff:** Champions collect points when they advocate for us. They can trade these points in for rewards, such as PowerDMS swag.

Advocate marketing can boost your referrals, reviews, and references. But it shouldn't just be about numbers. To succeed with advocate marketing, you must focus on building relationships."

—RAY LAU, CUSTOMER ADVOCACY MARKETING MANAGER, POWERDMS

"At WebPT, creating raving fans is one of our eight company values. The importance of this value is something that is well understood by each employee, discussed frequently by management and executives, and incorporated into decision-making. Culture can't be forced; you have to live it!"

—EMILY ELY, MEMBER MARKETING SPECIALIST, WEBPT

The Art and Practice of Advocate Marketing

The thought leader. The maverick. The trailblazer. It occurred to Deena a few years ago that pushing the boundaries as an early adopter can be a lonely and sometimes perilous position. You are looking left, while your colleagues are still looking right. You see a better way, but your org chart or budget does not. It's almost too easy to be labeled a rabble-rouser by the contented. For some, however, change is worth pursuing at almost any cost. The status quo is not an option.

The idea that as marketers we can positively impact the lives of people, instead of blasting out emails and dreaming up catchy tag lines, seems almost virtuous—working for *people*, rather than The Man. We are still fascinated by the *practice of advocacy*, even as we enter into a more mainstream era where the voice of the customer is now firmly central to success.

The intersection of relationship and result is the easiest way to sum up what advocate marketers are all about. Companies are driven by results—no surprise there. Where advocacy does depart from traditional marketing is in the *how*. How do you drive results when your customers are not personally driven by your outcomes?

Think about it: Have you ever bolted out of bed and pumped your fists in the air while wildly proclaiming with the pride of a lion: "I can't *wait* to give Company X a stellar referral or online review today!"?

Customers, when reframed as actual people and not personas, are driven by highly individualized and varied intrinsic and extrinsic goals. To complicate matters further for modern marketers, these desires span the personal-professional divide. Their motivations are endless and can change on a dime. There is one element, however, that can be refined with each and every customer, and, if ignored, can derail even the most well-articulated marketing efforts: *relationship*.

At a time when marketers must put aside their own telling of the brand story and turn up the dial on the *customer's* brand story, the advocate marketer flourishes. Hitting key goals, executing on well-designed marketing plans, contributing to the pipeline—these are the milestones of any marketer. What sets the advocate marketer apart is that achieving KPIs comes as an effect of building incredible, abiding, authentic relationships with customers, and raising those customers up in their own careers as a result.

The 80/20 rule applies here. Instead of spending 80 percent of the time building, deploying, and gating content, and 20 percent of the time thinking about who is interacting with that content, the advocate marketer does the opposite. Think of the advocate marketer as a sort of air traffic controller within your organization. They serve as the intermediary between the goals of your business and the goals of your customers. They work tirelessly to connect all departments, all projects, all organizational goals to your customers, translating from corporate speak to everyday conversations about interesting opportunities.

They are relatable, reliable relationship-building experts. They don't just know what products your customers use and why; they know when a baby is due, when a promotion happens, when a birthday is celebrated. They don't greet your customers with a stodgy handshake; they initiate an embrace. Over time, their interactions are real. They are meaningful. *The advocate marketer humanizes your business.*

ADVOCACY IN ACTION: STAPLES

Why would an office supply company need advocates? Their business isn't complicated. Everyone understands that people need office supplies, and the Staples brand is well established. What good could an advocacy program do?

Mary-Leslie Davis, Director of Field Marketing and Customer Engagement at Staples Business Advantage, understood that the benefits of developing customer advocacy for Staples' B2B business unit would outweigh the initial hesitation of her naysayers.

As part of Business Advantage's shift from a product-centric to a customer-centric marketing strategy, the team completed in-depth persona research to better understand their buyers. They discovered that every persona had one thing in common: the primary influence in purchasing decisions was word of mouth and peer references.

The advocate program pilot at Staples Business Advantage created a space for advocates to connect with each other, learn new success strategies, and gain recognition for their activity. In return for these benefits, they were given opportunities to advocate for the brand and answer questions or surveys for use throughout the business.

The discussion board, which allowed customers to foster direct con-nections, was one of the most valuable parts of the program. They enjoyed the opportunity to talk to each other, as many felt alone in their own organizations. Advocates loved the program so much, they were eager to support Staples Business Advantage any way they could and were happy to provide testimonials, case studies, and guest blogs. The most valuable result, however, was a pool of consumer insights, which the program surfaced.

"Here was a way I could talk to and hear what my customers were saying every single day," says Mary-Leslie. "Our advocacy program became a rich source of customer insight. Salespeople talk to customers all the time, but those of us who sit in corporate head-quarters talk to customers *maybe* once or twice a year. I wanted to find an avenue where we could talk to customers on a daily basis without doing some big fancy research project that's put on the shelf after you finish it. And then I wanted our customers to turn around and talk about us!"

The early pilot program proved to have impact across the business. With the advocacy program, her team:

- Helped the ecommerce group find volunteers within the community to test new functionality
- Settled a weeks-long debate for the internal creative agency of a campaign by posing a quick poll to the advocate community, and provided a clear winner within hours.
- Let the strategy team test new products and services to understand how they'd resonate with customers. Value propositions and proof points could be validated quickly, sparing the organization from reliance on gut feelings, or the need to hire a research firm to source insights
- Helped merchandising make faster decisions based on advocate feedback
- Identified potential sales opportunities for the sales team through buying signals indicated by a community member's activity on the discussion board

The naysayers proven wrong, Mary-Leslie's next challenge was to prove ROI to expand the advocate program internally. She analyzed the sales stemming from highly engaged advocates, and found that they spent significantly more than other top customers.

She successfully got the funding to move forward.

"Now we have a real-time view of what our customers are thinking and what's top of mind. This equips us to create valuable case studies and whitepapers that speak directly to their needs. These insights allow us to drive strategy for the whole company."

RELATIONSHIP-OBTAINED INVESTMENT: THE NEW ROI

Think about your company's total investment in customer relationships today. What are you bringing to the table? What are you receiving in return? By reframing relationships as currency, we become more mindful about how the investment appreciates over time, and how the investment can lose value if it's not carefully managed. Each time you ask an advocate to participate, you are essentially making a withdrawal from your investment. Give your investments time to grow, and never overspend.

Be meticulous about minding the balance between what's in it for you and what's in it for them. Advocates will be ready, willing, and able to answer calls for any number of asks, but how much is too much? How much is not enough? In our currency analogy, overdrawing occurs when you rely on too few advocates too often. This is a behavior change for many of us who are used to going to our key contacts repeatedly—after all, they are known, vetted, and ready to go. Seems like a low risk, right? However, in doing so, the opportunity to develop relationships with the myriad other advocates whose stories have yet to be told is lost.

TAKING THE TIME TO LISTEN

Active advocacy can take time, and the time of your advocates must be highly valued. Be generous with small perks;

take the time and budget to offer incentives and member benefits that are meaningful and aspirational. Spend your budget wisely by aligning spend with community goals. This way, you incentivize action on the exact activities that are most meaningful to your business.

Every interaction should be meaningful. Just like you, advocates are typically strapped for time. This means any time they spend advocating for your company should be treated with a white glove; you must offer something relevant to the advocate each and every time they interact with your company and community. Whether it's a new opportunity or new incentive, new discussion or new best practice, every interaction must be curated with the advocate in mind. The key here is to be mindful of time. Don't ask too much, too often.

Do something with everything you're given. Taking action on the time your advocates give you is critical. Don't ask your advocates to undertake an activity unless you have a plan or a goal supporting that ask. If you appear to waste the advocate's time, you may not have the chance to do so ever again. Every question and every activity should have a follow-up action. There must always be a reason for advocacy, even if the reason is simply to listen.

When you spend more time listening than talking, you'll

learn about your advocates. Knowing if someone prefers a latte over an Americano may sound like a minor detail, but the next time you see that person and you arrive with an Americano in hand, you have just expertly crafted a moment that matters. The opportunities to surprise and delight are the cornerstone of the expert advocate marketer. Delights can include sending a spa certificate to a new mother; a pizza party for the advocate's team in his or her office; an upgraded room at a conference. Many of these are small, budget-friendly tokens of appreciation. Most of the time, the gestures have no direct impact on your program goals, but rather are an investment in the relationship. The cumulative effect of such moments serves to deepen the advocate's affinity for your company and brand.

Listening to the community is the key to bringing them on board. The primary reason people initially join a community—especially an online community related to a company—is the desire to provide feedback. They want to be heard.

ADVOCACY IN ACTION: PEARSON

College students know the name Pearson—they're the textbook vendors.

Pearson thinks of itself as the world's largest learning company, which additionally offers technology, materials, and services to help students reach their full potential. Why isn't *that* common knowledge?

Pearson needed to change the way students perceived their brand, so they turned to social advocacy, and found stunning success.

Lindsey Erlick, Senior Manager of Student Advocacy & Marketing at Pearson, knew they needed to build brand affinity and wanted students to know that Pearson is more than just textbooks. They made it a top priority to put students at the center of everything they did.

In February 2016, the company launched an advocate marketing program (using Influitive's AdvocateHub platform) to drive student advocacy, loyalty, and engagement.

The program, called the Pearson Student Insiders, is an exclusive student community that gives members special opportunities, resources, and perks for building their employability skills and engaging with Pearson. This helps the company build stronger relationships with students and collect valuable insights to inform their products and marketing.

Within a year of launching the program, Pearson:

- Dramatically improved their brand sentiment among students in the program
- Filled their daily blog with student-created content—three months in advance
- Grew the community to more than 3,100 college students who are now better prepared to find internships and employment after graduation
- Collected 3,250-plus pieces of student feedback to inform product and program development
- Boosted content and social media engagement metrics

"We doubled our mentions and positive sentiment within a month of launching," said Lindsey. "Our social media team was shocked and wanted to know what we were doing."

Lindsey knew the marketing team wanted to improve brand sentiment and uncover more student stories, while the product team needed more user feedback. She made the program's top goal to raise Pearson's brand perception among college students, increasing content creation and collecting more product feedback. To do this, she set a goal to mobilize 1,000 student advocates by May of that same year. To start, they targeted their happiest users, who had expressed an interest in interacting with them.

"About 800,000 college students use our products," said Lindsey. "When we initially invited advocates to join the Pearson Student Insiders program, we narrowed it down to students who gave us a high Net Promoter Score, and had opted in to hear about our programs through web surveys."

When new advocates joined the Pearson Student Insiders program, they were surveyed about their interests and which products they used. Lindsey then created segments so she could target specific student groups with relevant content and requests. This was helpful when the product team wanted to hear from students in certain majors who used certain products.

She hosted monthly video talks in which students chatted about their challenges and interests. These talks allowed Pearson and students to exchange ideas and learn from each other. Early on, she also provided her advocates with professional development content, such as tips on building their resumes and networking.

Before the Student Insiders program, Pearson's product development team didn't have a central system for collecting meaningful student feedback. Lindsey asked students to take polls, join focus groups, and serve as beta testers through the program. Within a year, Pearson received more than 3,250 student responses.

These insights have helped Pearson put students at the heart of every decision they make, and has helped students understand that Pearson values their opinions.

Before asking for something big, such as an entire blog written by advocates, Lindsey first asked what topics interested the Pearson Student Insiders. Then she asked them to pitch their own blog ideas.

"Before launching the program, we got about forty pitches per semester," says Lindsey. "This past year, we've received almost 1,200 blog pitches from students across North America. The Insiders program has enabled us to reach out to more students and give them the opportunity to tell their story."

Within the past year, Pearson has published more than 300 student blog posts.

Pearson's blog comments and social shares have also increased, as advocates relate to the student-created content and want to support other Insiders. In the past, Pearson received one to ten comments per month across all of their student blogs. Now, they get ten to twenty comments per month.

Pearson also doubled their social engagement from advocate stories—generating 4,114 social shares over the past year.

This has helped Pearson:

- Increase post reach by 10 percent
- Boost post engagement by 5 percent
- Increase conversion rates and clicks on their blog posts by 5 percent
- Get thirty video testimonials and seventy written testimonials from students

When advocates help you out, it's important to let them know they're appreciated. This way, they'll continue to advocate in the future.

"You want to create a reason for people to come back," said Lindsey.

To make Pearson's advocates feel valued, she gave them a shout-out on social media or sent them a customized video whenever they helped out the brand or achieved success, like acing an exam.

Lindsey didn't always have the time to speak one-on-one with every advocate, so she created special badges and points that automatically rewarded advocates when they completed a task. They could redeem points for special perks, or gain clout on the community leaderboard.

Within a year of launching the Pearson Student Insiders program, Pearson engaged more than 3,100 college advocates. Lindsey also achieved her goal of improving Pearson's brand perception.

"Our Insiders no longer see us as a big, faceless company," says Lindsey. "Instead, they see us as friends who can help them succeed in their careers."

She wants to help more students succeed. With more than 19 million college students in the United States, she sees endless possibilities for growth.

"Before, we had no way to give students access or show that we wanted their input," said Lindsey. "Now, we can easily tap into our ever-growing list of advocates."

THE POWER OF ACTIVE LISTENING

Seth Lieberman, CEO of SnapApp, talked about the power of listening at Advocamp 2016. He said:

> Active listening is mission-critical. One of the most important things about great experiences and about customer conversations is that they are dialogues, where most marketing is a monologue. Stephen Covey has a fantastic quote that I love: "Most people do not listen with the intent to understand. They listen with the intent to reply."
>
> This is really true if you work with sales teams. The first thing they are thinking when they are in a conversation is, "What should I say back? What should I answer?" What you really should be saying is, "What is the problem? You're saying this, but is that what you really mean?"
>
> Marketers have to learn how to be active listeners, so we can understand what problems customers are facing, and really understand what motivates advocates.

Once we start to actively listen, we can create great experiences. Here is a great experience: has anybody ever taken a trolley car? It is great, but it is less good than an Uber, right? An Uber comes on demand anywhere I am, is super convenient, and takes me anywhere I want to go for less than any other price. That is part of a great experience.

The second thing is that you have to be personal. Knowledge and intimacy drive brand, credibility, and trust. This is really powerful, but it's only done if we're listening to what matters and delivering great experiences.

TOTAL CONTROL IS NOT THE OBJECTIVE

Feedback comes in different qualities—some helpful, some not. If the information isn't honest, it isn't useful. When you solicit feedback from your advocates, how do you know that you're getting honest feedback?

Leaders, as well as colleagues and other stakeholders, can hesitate to ask for feedback, because they assume advocates will simply tell them what they want to hear. That's why it's important to pay more than lip service to listening; companies that succeed *actually* listen, even if the feedback they hear isn't the feedback they want. Listening to challenging feedback along with the great feedback is the key to demonstrating authenticity as a company.

Over the past several decades, the marketing profession has built a persona of a drill sergeant with a bullhorn, yelling its message indiscriminately and unrelentingly. The bullhorn approach doesn't work as well today. People demand authenticity and reciprocation. Marketers need to think of themselves more like orchestra conductors: they don't make the music themselves, they elicit it from others.

Rather than broadcasting from a megaphone, marketers need to encourage others to go out and carry their message. That might mean losing some degree of control. The message may not always be exactly what they want it to be, but it will be more authentic, and will resonate with a wider variety of people. An orchestra can produce more sound—and a more beautiful sound—than a bullhorn.

It's exciting to see the success of companies like OnePlus. To go from zero to $300 million in less than a year with no marketing budget is astounding. This is the future of marketing.

Young marketers of today, early in their careers, experience success that many of us could never have dreamed of because they've learned to market this way. These "beginners" get to interact with the top people in their organization and immediately take their careers to the next level.

Learn to listen and learn what to do next. You've listened to what your advocates want and need; how do you deliver it? How do you surprise and delight in your delivery? Companies organized around advocates sometimes make different decisions about how they invest in products. There's often not a one-to-one return on investment, but delighting your users now pays massive dividends long-term.

THE MAGIC OF SMALL TOUCHES

One accounting program we use at Influitive includes a delightful image of a big robot hand stamping "paid" on an invoice. It took time to design that image and implement it within the design of the application—yet the graphic itself has no function. What is the return on that investment of time? No product manager can reasonably claim that in paying X number of dollars to a designer to create an image, the company will make Y number of dollars in return. It simply can't be measured that directly. However, we, and other users of the software, are enchanted by the robot hand. It's a tiny touch that is memorable and delightful. It's what we remember when we think of the brand. That memory is the key to inspiring advocacy and devotion.

Apple delights users with the unboxing experience. Tesla includes a "bio-weapon defense mode" in their car—an air filter—and drivers get a kick out of the label. When users are thrilled with these seemingly small touches, they talk about it with other people, who also talk about it, creating a buzz.

It doesn't take much to see a huge return on advocacy. With just a 12 percent increase in advocacy, on average, a company can experience a 2X growth in revenue, according to a report in the Harvard Business School Press.[20] Pay attention to the little touches that build the magic of your brand; it's what advocates remember, and what they most want to talk about.

ADVOCATE COMMUNITIES

Buzz is created in communities where advocates build their own communities. Companies can take some actions to encourage community building, but advocates also do their own thing. We've seen that at Influitive: advocates have created their own local communities and online user groups that are completely beyond our control. Deena once asked if she could attend an advocate marketing meetup put on by one such group. They politely replied in the negative, pointing out that it was strictly for members.

You can support advocate communities by providing a central, supportive place to work from, but they'll often take the ball and run with it from there. As your advocate

---

20 https://influitive.com/dictionary/advocacy-marketing/

community grows, you will likely have to relinquish some level of control to allow it to flourish.

Ultimately, we want advocacy to happen on its own. We provide a central place, but we encourage the smaller pockets of advocacy that build off themselves to become satellite programs. The secret is to stay as hands-off as possible, and only step in if invited.

THE PSYCHOLOGY OF COMMUNITY

How can you inspire members to join and take part in your advocate community? Let's look at six reasons why people tend to join and participate in groups:[21]

1. To tackle a problem they're aware of (or intuitively feel)

There are two parts of this. First, you need to tackle a problem that requires them to frequently participate. Single-topic problems don't work well. Tackle a bigger life issue, one that is part of a bigger puzzle.

This will usually be something that affects our health, wealth, or happiness. Members might ask about the best running shoes in a community about running shoes, but ask most questions in a fitness community.

---

21 https://www.feverbee.com/participate-2/

Second, members must already know they have this problem and want to solve it. It's almost impossible to make members aware of a problem they don't already know about.

The problem must be something that matters to them. If you ask members about their biggest challenges and they don't mention the problem, don't build a community around this topic.

2. To take advantage of an opportunity they believe exists

A growing number of communities are catered to helping members take advantage of an opportunity that may now exist. BackpackingLight is an example of this. Every backpacker knows there is new technology out there to lighten their backpacks; they just need a place to go for it.

Many members of CommunityGeek join because they know they could be doing more to use psychology and data to grow communities.

Opportunities usually come from changes in the political, economic, social, or technological sectors.[22] These create new opportunities people need to make sense of.

---

22 PEST Analysis, http://www.businessballs.com/freepdfmaterials/pest-analysis-free-template.pdf

They are usually places where you want to do something quicker, cheaper, faster, or better. You can't create the opportunity, but you can use Google Trends to identify rising opportunities and encapsulate them as the basis for your community.

3. To pursue an existing interest

People join communities if they want to learn more about a topic they're fascinated by; most hobbyist and enthusiast communities fall within this category. Many brands try to create communities in this field, but soon realize that their brand isn't nearly as fascinating as they might expect.

These communities are very hard to create, because the majority of them already exist. New ones, provoked by PEST, may come about, but these opportunities are rare, and difficult for organizations to facilitate.

Still, you can identify opportunities by asking your members what percentage of their free time they spend engaged in enthusiast discussion and activities. If enough members spend significant weekly time—three hours or more—bonding with other fans, you've identified an opportunity to create a new community.

4. To be a part of a known exclusive group

People are wired to join exclusive groups within their fields; it boosts their social standing and signals their value. Many companies, however, mistake *exclusive* for *secret*.

Secret groups are far less effective, because the element of social signaling is necessarily absent. The most effective exclusive groups are those most people know exist, but can't join. If you have an exclusive group, it's a good idea to promote it.

5. To avoid the fear of missing out

Once a community has achieved critical mass, an increasing number of people join so as not to be left behind. This happens in communities like Reddit and ProductHunt, which achieve incredibly high levels of growth and participation.

At this stage, it's a good idea to promote the high levels of growth, success stories, and the community's metadata. If your community is wildly successful, promote that success.

6. To satisfy personal ego needs

Many people join a community to satisfy an immediate need for validation or efficacy. They join to write a provocative remark and see others agree with them. They aim to see an impact and know they have efficacy within the community and agency over their actions.

Others join to share a useful piece of advice. They want to be congratulated and feel validated that they have expertise in the topic.

These are usually the least healthy communities. YouTube comments might be the most obvious example: the typical comments section is an echo chamber of ego. These are specifically the kinds of members and activity you *don't* want in your community.

COMMUNITY STRATEGY

The best strategies filter out as many weak opportunities as possible to focus on a few single, decisive areas. In a community context, you need to find the best way to achieve your objectives above.

A strategy is the emotion that will change the behavior of your target audience. This means that, in order to write a great strategy, you need first to understand what changes behavior. This is where we need to understand a little more about psychology.

Facts are far less powerful than emotions when it comes to

changing member behavior. Think about climate change: most people believe that climate change is both manmade and a serious threat to this planet, yet few people have changed their ways.

Behavior change is achieved by amplifying specific emotions to evoke a shift in actions.

The best community strategy, therefore, is the science of amplifying emotions to change the behavior of a specific group of people. A good community strategy begins with identifying the emotion you want to amplify within the group.

Remember, too, that you will need at least one strategy for your priority objectives, and a unique strategy for your failsafe objectives. If you are lucky, the strategies will closely align. In practice, it is more likely that you will need to pursue two relatively distinct strategies for different target audiences.

FROM "BADVOCATES" TO ADVOCATES

Remaining involved in the communities you create, even if from a distance, is crucially important. If you don't provide some direction, people are going to take matters into their own hands, and their decisions could be to your detriment. Like it or not, there are "badvocate" communities out there.

Airlines experience this, with online groups dedicated to complaining about bad service on flights. These groups are usually just looking to be heard, and have found solidarity and validation in the shared suffering of other customers like them.

One constructive way to hear these customers is to pull them into your advocacy strategy. A financial services company, for example, saw badvocates forming groups because of their disenchantment with the company. Counterintuitively, they decided to pull the complainers into their advocacy program. They got the disgruntled customers connected to product managers and turned them around.

The customers who seek you out to say they're upset, and want you to do something about it, sincerely care. They're passionate. They want to be heard. That's the stuff raving fans are made of. Don't ignore them. Funnel them into positive communities; surround them with people who are having a positive experience with you, such as a customer who has recently had a tough support ticket resolved, or who had product issues but their ranting resulted in a product innovation, or a tough renewal customer who is now seeing value.

Here are some examples of this strategy at play:

A customer actually reached out to me *before* leaving a Google review. He called support and asked to be connected to me directly. He said he respected what I was doing and wanted to give me a chance to fix his problem before he let it out online. First thought: how the hell am I going to fix a technical issue? After sitting on the phone with him for 30 minutes listening to his complaint, I went over to the support team and they were already on top of it. He ended up leaving us a decent review saying we had timely response to issues.

EMILIA JANCZAK, SOCIAL MEDIA
MARKETING MANAGER, EVOLVE IP

Not everyone in our advocacy program loves us. We have one advocate who is neutral and sometimes negative. She posted an average Google review, so I reached out to her to see how we could improve it and find out why she has a neutral attitude about us.

JESSICA MITCHELL, CUSTOMER
MARKETING MANAGER, HERO K12

Communities help the advocate marketer scale up the program. If the group members are active, the marketer doesn't have to manage so many people directly. Again, it's like conducting an orchestra, only in this case you have some additional conductors you can depend on to manage even more players. Consider asking an advocate to moderate a community forum; have an advocate host weekly Twitter chats or a local community meet-up.

DON'T FORGET: YOU ARE A MEMBER, TOO

What sets advocate marketing apart from other forms of customer engagement is a true investment in your relationship with the customer. The advocate must feel trusted and valued in order to reap the most benefit from their interactions with you, and you from them. Think about this in terms of your personal life: your most fruitful and abiding relationships are those which you constantly nurture, those which you focus your time and energy on with intention.

To be most effective, your marketing focus is best rooted in an authentic desire to help your customers be more successful. If an advocate senses that your program is not genuinely about them and their own motivations, you will lose their support. Worse still, you may not have the chance to get it back. You must be *authentically* interested in their success. Your advocate's success *is your success*. The more access to education, tools, resources and opportunities they have related to their professional mission, the more successful they are, and the greater the chances are of a stronger, stickier implementation of your product or service. Think of this as *mutually assured success.*

Just as you are asking your advocates to champion your business or brand, you must reciprocate. The relationship requires balance and mutual benefit. If your customer advocate has a key win in their professional or personal life, make sure you celebrate it. Write their boss an email, or feature their story in a newsletter or blog.

Whatever and whenever appropriate, be your advocate's biggest advocate.

IMMEDIATELY IMPROVE THE LIVES OF YOUR CUSTOMERS

"Help them build their professional brands and grow with their company through training and certifications."
—MICHAEL BEAHM, SENIOR MARKETING MANAGER, BLACKBAUD

"You have a problem? We have a solution—and really mean that mantra. If we do not have a product or solution in our wheel-house that works for your problem, we will work with you to create that solution. Making it more than just about a sale proves to be a truly remarkable impact."
—LAURA OLSON, CORPORATE MARKETING MANAGER, DOCUSIGN

"Always provide an excellent solution when customers state their problems or issues. Customers like to feel that their word has been heard, so always pay attention to their needs and provide a quickly and accurate solution. Listen to their concerns."
—SARAH CUBAS, CONSULTANT

Integrating Advocacy

So, where do you start?

The first thing a company can do to get started on an advocate marketing program is adopt an advocacy mindset. Your company needs to be built around the value of advocacy. That's the end goal for the best companies—discovering, nurturing, and mobilizing advocates—because it works, and will continue to work in the future.

Many companies who have never heard the term *advocate marketing* currently do some level of advocate engagement, often without even realizing it; where they fall short is in follow-through. They ask the questions, but fail to integrate the answers.

Consider a company we worked with at Influitive. When they came to us, they had already implemented a feedback system; they ask their customers if they'd recommend them to others on an annual or semi-annual Net Promoter Score, or NPS, survey. This survey measures the loyalty that exists between a company and its customers.

Sending the NPS survey regularly was a stellar first step. However, the furthest this company leveraged the data they received was simply to note their Net Promoter Score and use it as a benchmark for the next NPS survey deployed months later.

Why wouldn't you ask your 9s and 10s how else they'd like to engage with your company, and take advantage of their enthusiasm? With those scores, those customers are telling you that they are *already* advocates. Ask those promoters if they're interested in providing a sales reference, sharing their story in a case study, speaking on an upcoming webinar, or submitting an online review. Show them you are listening, and that you deeply value their opinions.

Furthermore, what about 7s and 8s? There is huge potential to nurture those customers through an advocate marketing program to turn their sentiment about your company from good to great. It's not only about improving their sentiment; it's about improving your business processes and products to better meet the expectations of your customers, and cultivate an army of advocates along the way.

NPS is a common first step, but exceptional companies go further by leveraging every intersection with their happy customers as a potential advocate-recruiting and advocacy-generating opportunity. By valuing every opportunity and measuring everything related to advocate engagement, you turn relationships into currency.

A CEO recently told us that his company measures *time to advocacy* for each new customer. They want to know how long it takes for a customer to become an enthusiastic, active advocate. It isn't enough for the customer to develop the intention to act; they *must* act. To measure time to advocacy, this company invites customers to give a video testimonial or get on stage to talk about the company. When they're ready to do that, they're true advocates.

WHERE AN ORGANIZATION'S ADVOCACY JOURNEY BEGINS

Businesses have two mindsets concerning customers: the Transactional Mindset and the Advocacy Mindset.

The Transactional Mindset is simple: relationships with customers are viewed as finite, quid-pro-quo entities.

The Advocacy Mindset is the belief that true, long-term advocacy from your customers is driven by a mutually beneficial relationship. Embracing this concept means that the first question you need to ask yourself about any advocacy program you build is not, "What's in it for us?" But rather, "What's in it for *them?*"

Similar to the start of a relationship, the focus when inviting customers to an advocacy program should be heavily weighted toward bringing value to the other participant. The Advocacy Mindset begins to develop the moment you introduce advocacy to your organization.[23] [24]

Why: Transactional vs Relational Advocacy Model

Transactional advocacy models can produce near-term results but rarely see long-term success.

23   Liz Richardson. *The Advocate Marketer's Companion.*

24   Deena Zenyk, Liz Richardson.

HOW TO CREATE THE ADVOCACY MINDSET

"We focus on delivering a best-in-class experience for our clients. When that occurs, we are likely to have clients want to advocate on our behalf. Without the underlying successful service experience, true advocacy won't exist."

—SARAH LAMB, SR. STRATEGY ANALYST AT ADP

"Truly realize that your success as a company is dependent on your customers, and do things to support, nurture and grow that. Don't leave it up to chance!"

—RAY LAU, CUSTOMER ADVOCACY MARKETING

MANAGER AT POWERDMS

BUILDING A SOLID FOUNDATION: INTERNAL READINESS

Once you have instilled your intention to build an advocacy mindset within your organization, there arises the more difficult next step: getting key stakeholders and employees on board.

First, work on gathering allies. Developing a network of internal advocacy supporters early and often is key to the success of a truly cross-departmental program. Often, this starts with a key champion in a position to provide budget and make decisions, such as director or VP/CMO/CXO. You will need to intimately understand your champion's key drivers for supporting advocacy and deliver on those metrics.

Understanding who should be interested in advocacy is the next critical step. Many of your colleagues will not yet have an in-depth understanding of the power of advocacy. It will be up to you to educate, initiative, and cultivate a team around you who share a passion for your customers, their stories, and developing a relationship with them that is genuine. While many advocacy programs are managed by a single resource, there is value in bringing key colleagues into the fold as part of a cross-departmental advisory committee. This will help you keep on top of opportunities for your advocates outside of your immediate department, and further entrench the value of advocacy across the organization.

Next, in order to avoid positioning advocacy as *just another program* that your colleagues are being asked to support, ensure to connect advocacy directly to their own goals and objectives. Most organizations offer some visibility in the goals and objectives of other departments. Find out what the drivers are for customer success, product management and development, training and professional development, marketing, and sales.

Once you have established your internal advocacy landscape, it's time to set up small cross-departmental group meetings to do the following:

1. Educate on what advocacy is and why it is important to your business as a whole
2. Facilitate a workshop based on the individual stakeholders' goals

You'll want to demonstrate exactly how advocacy can positively impact each person in their role. Remember: *Advocacy can help your colleagues exceed their goals.* An internal roadshow approach to building momentum around advocacy will help you to deliver a multi-faceted program to your advocates; some of whom will be more interested in impacting product development, and others who will be more interested in speaking opportunities, for example.

TIP

Map your organization of internal stakeholders and champions. Aim for allies at both the contributor and management levels, and ensure you have executive buy-in at every step of your foundation building.

Then, create a table that maps their individual and departmental goals and objectives. You'll need to understand these key indicators as a motivation for your colleagues to support your program.

Once you have established who is working toward what goals, set up your series of internal roadshow meetings. It's important to customize your approach and content based on who is attending the meeting.

CREATE YOUR ADVOCACY STORYLINE

To best promote your advocacy program within your organization, you must become the internal subject matter expert on all things advocacy. As such, you will also be the primary *advocacy storyteller*. It is important that the advocacy portfolio is understood by your internal stakeholders in two key ways:

1. Via the stories of the customers you will invite into the program
2. Via stories that will connect to the internal stakeholders' goals and objectives

This means you may need to create more than one advocacy storyline, and you may need to tell these stories via different channels. For example, let's say you begin your storytelling with the sales team. Your story must focus on the benefits to the sales organization, and key past wins where customers helped accelerate or close deals. Channels for a sales story might include a sales kickoff meeting, a sales portal or intranet, or a weekly or monthly sales call.

Once you've met with your internal stakeholders and have helped them connect advocacy to their own goals, it's time to create a broader plan that levels up from there. Whether you are using a spreadsheet or a more advanced planning software, the intended outcome is the same: you need a bird's-eye view of all the key milestones across stakeholder departments. Once you have this visual, you will likely find linear connections between these milestones that you can leverage to your advantage.

Here's a look at a possible bird's-eye view within your company:

Product development delivers a new product. Then, product marketing develops materials for a go-to-market strategy. These materials impact sales as they prepare to sell, and marketing as they prepare to market. At each of these stages, there is an intersection with advocacy.

The developers need advocates to test and refine the product; product marketing needs advocates to test messaging and develop personas; sales needs advocates who have touched the product to act as references; and marketing needs advocates for case studies, press releases, webinars, blog posts, and social sharing of all the new product materials.

Your 12-month plan may have 6 or more key milestones. It's your job to figure out how you can mobilize your advocates around each of them, and at every intersection along the way. Your internal stakeholders might not have advocacy top-of-mind, or fully understand exactly all the ways advocates can help. You need to surface these intersections often and report on the results of the interactions.

TIE ADVOCATE MARKETING INTO BROADER INITIATIVES

Your program goals might include metrics around new joins to the program, pipeline influence, and social influence/impact. These are typical goals. You need to level these goals up and find attachment points to the broader initiatives in your company. Tie your goals into these key milestones, and be relentless in ensuring that the impact the advocacy program has had in relation to these milestones is noted and reported.

SHARE YOUR RESULTS INTERNALLY

Consider reporting up and out on a bi-weekly or monthly basis. Share the hard-and-fast metrics of your advocacy program, and, most crucially, the *good news* stories. Tie your advocates' stories to your program plan and your metrics.

Where you report is often as important as *how* you report; don't stick with a simple email. Think about who in your company most needs to see and absorb the reporting; then figure out where these stakeholders go for information. Is there an intranet? A newsletter? A monthly alignment meeting? A town hall? Digital signage in your head office? Explore all reporting avenues, then modify what you report and when you report on it based on the audience and the reporting venue.

Above all, be persistent, tenacious, and relentless in your reporting. Leave no potential avenue for sharing your success and the successes of your advocates unexplored. Reporting should be a significant slice of your monthly workflow.

CELEBRATE WITH YOUR ADVOCATES!

Happiness begets happiness, in life and in advocate marketing. Sharing the accomplishments of your advocates and your program will go a long way toward increasing affinity with your company, the advocate community, and your brand.

Celebrate milestones big and small. Share a wedding announcement with the community, then crowdsource ideas for an engagement gift. Share the good news of a promotion, then ask your advocates to share their congratulations with the recently promoted advocate. The more you celebrate—the more you focus on your advocates as real people—the stronger and longer-lasting your program will become.

LEVELING UP

What is the timeline within a company for adopting an advocacy mindset and institutional advocacy focus? It differs across the board, but we have seen patterns in advocacy program creation throughout the dozens of companies we've worked with. We have found that there are five levels a company moves through on its way to sustained growth and satisfaction with advocacy efforts.

LEVEL 1: AD HOC AND DIRECTIONLESS

A Level 1 organization is likely not recognizing that they're "doing" advocacy, yet they're already running a reference program or offer referral incentives. Perhaps they've asked a customer to be a guest speaker at an event, or have featured a customer success story in a case study or press release.

Although they don't yet have a clear plan, dedicated budget, or an employee responsible for advocate marketing, they have sporadic touch points with customers on an as-needed basis. There's little to no value placed on measuring value, and very little thought given to the advocate's experience or relationship with the company.

At this level, the company doesn't truly understand the advocate marketing concept yet. Some of it happens at an individual level—such as sales reps drumming up referrals—but there's no organized program.

LEVEL 2: NARROW AND REACTIVE

A Level 2 company has likely embarked on their advocacy journey and is starting to make some investment in advocate marketing, like a dedicated community or program run by a part-time headcount. At this level, advocate marketing tends to be positioned in a marketing department and supports existing departmental goals, such as content creation.

Level 2 programs are not highly strategic, nor well-diffused across the organization, but they open the door to select cross-departmental stakeholders to connect with advocates and learn more about them.

At this stage of development, the advocate experience tends to be transactional, and there is no actionable strategic plan being followed. There is little to no focus on nurturing authentic relationships.

A Level 2 company may have an advocate program and do some things to generate advocacy, but it's a loose program, probably more of an island off to the side of marketing. It may not be well-integrated, and may lack useful metrics, but it's a start.

LEVEL 3: MANAGED AND COORDINATED

Companies at Level 3 have advocacy programs that are more strategic, better staffed and funded, and more visible within the organization. Level 3s have learned about their advocates, and now curate a highly personalized experience for them while engaging with them in meaningful ways. Discovery and nurturing of advocates is ongoing, a precursor to meaningful, longer-term mobilization.

At this level, an advocate marketing brand is emerging, and the recruitment of advocates from broader audiences is typical. The program is evolving to be more relationship-driven than purely transactional.

Level 3 companies have started to broaden their marketing to include advocates. Their advocate program reaches out beyond traditional marketing functions; everything that happens in marketing is interwoven with public relations, demand generation, and advertising. Whatever the marketing department does, they integrate customer advocates as part of the way they go to market. They're no longer alone on an island.

LEVEL 4: EXPANDED AND PERVASIVE

A Level 4 company has advocate marketing that goes beyond the marketing department. They heavily leverage advocates to figure out what they should build and how they should build it. They get the voice of the customer involved in how they innovate. They have customer success functions that leverage advocates to generate renewals and upsells. They measure their success in actual advocacy, not just promised advocacy.

The Level 4 organization has a highly strategic advocate marketing platform in place that connects advocates with their business and with their peers. Another hallmark of a business operating at this level is the technical integration of advocate marketing into other systems and tools.

Operating on a highly strategic fiscal-year plan, advocate marketing is an established key business driver with the staff to support it. The accountability for advocate marketing includes a senior-level executive and at least one additional full-time dedicated and experienced resource. Its value is understood by executives and other departments—product, customer success, and sales, for instance—as delivering measurable value across the organization. Increasingly, advocates cross paths with individual contributors in various departments, and have access to the company's executives.

At this stage of maturity, the investment in offline engagements grows as the program's reach beyond marketing is understood and actioned. The advocate experience with a Level 4 business is highly personalized, personally beneficial, and there's a sense of a mutually beneficial peer network between members.

In a Level 4 company, the sales department actively encourages advocacy during the prospect's buying process. They work with others across the organization. The prospective customer might speak not just to a sales rep, but also to their peers. Communication with potential advocates becomes part of a Level 4 company's organization across multiple departments, but isn't quite an organizational imperative yet.

LEVEL 5: ADVOCATE-FIRST ORGANIZATIONAL IMPERATIVE

This is the promised land of advocate marketing: its scope and value extend across and throughout the business in its entirety. The discipline of advocate marketing now has its own department, with multiple levels of seniority and initiatives in place to support key company objectives. With a significant budget, the long-range strategic advocate marketing plan includes a balance of offline and online engagement and a highly tailored experience across each customer's journey.

Advocates experience significant professional growth

because of their participation in the program. A subset of advocates emerges from the community as trusted advisors and thought leaders. Their endorsement is golden. The advocate marketing brand has developed to become recognizable in the industry, and advocates are so invested in the program they self-create grassroots sub-communities and connections that thrive outside of the program.

We call such highly evolved companies Level 5 companies because they've progressed through the four levels of the following maturity model:

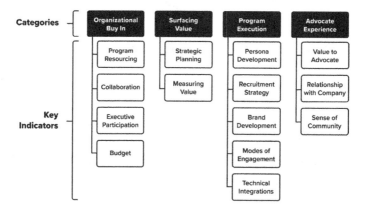

ADVANCING TO LEVEL 5

When we start working with companies, they're typically at Level 2, with a rudimentary advocacy program in place. They may have a referral program, take surveys, and ask for customer stories, but those things aren't necessarily well integrated. These are often mid-market companies, with around 250 employees. They understand that advocacy work is important, but know they could be doing it better.

Often, Influitive will be brought in when a new head of marketing begins work and is excited to grow the company. Bigger companies may even have a VP of customer advocacy, or similar position, but they're still largely focused on the marketing department. They may not even be leveraging advocacy for everything they do in marketing.

We work with these Level 2 companies to improve integration and metrics, and to make the program advocate-facing. It should be fun and rewarding. That's how we get them to Level 3, and on the path up to Level 5. As the company moves advocate marketing as a strategy to the center of the organization, they put themselves on a path to running an advocate-first business. There's more rigor involved, which permeates every department of the company. They start thinking of advocacy in sales, products, and human resources.

Our process at Influitive begins with an evaluation. We ask, "What are you doing today?"

Typically, companies reply, "Well, we've got this program where we try to get our customers to talk on stage, and we've got this other thing where we try to get referrals, and the sales department has a program where they need people to talk to prospects before they close deals…"

It's vague and fragmented. They've created these programs without a strategy, simply out of reactivity. They are focused only on accelerating the buyer's process. They know that referral leads are better than other leads, and that five-star reviews make people buy, so they've made five-star reviews their primary objective.

The next question we ask these folks is: "What's stopping you from doing more?"

Eventually, advocacy becomes a rallying point, an essential goal that employees shoot for. In a Level 5 company, everyone involved is primed to delight customers to the point where they become raving fans. The company can then derive the most value out of those fans. The process becomes part of the culture. Plus, it's more fun than what they were doing before! No one has to make cold calls to irritated prospects anymore; instead, they're providing an experience that make prospects happy. That makes everybody feel good.

A company we work with called aPriori embodies Level 5 thinking. Even though they are still small, with only a couple of people in marketing, every decision in the company is made based on how it can generate more advocates. aPriori is always thinking about how to make their advocates even more excited about what they're doing, and their advocates are, in turn, passionate promoters.

Here's the rub: aPriori makes product-costing software. When is the last time you were a raving fan of product-costing software?

This is proof of the fundamental truth about advocate marketing: it works no matter what your product is.

YOU GOT TO LEVEL 5: NOW, HOW TO STAY THERE?

Advocate marketing programs require care and feeding. Most advocacy programs don't die from overuse, but from neglect. People take for granted the enthusiastic return from their advocates, and they stop feeding the machine with moments of delight.

Keep offering your advocates interesting opportunities that enhance their lives and supercharge their careers. They will burn out if you keep asking for favors without delighting them. Think about how to make them feel like they're part of the tribe, that they're moving the meter, that they're gaining social capital. Advocate programs are like your company's muscles: use them or lose them.

Advocate marketing is not a silver bullet; it's a mindset. You don't set up a program and walk away. You must make the shift to thinking about the kinds of experiences buyers are looking for, then plan how to deliver those experiences in strategic alignment with your overall objectives. That isn't hard if you've seen firsthand how well it works.

We talked with one CEO whose mantra was, "I don't want to see any marketing going out without happy customers attached to it." He came to that perspective through a career in marketing that showed him that putting out hype just didn't work. The only thing that ever worked was happy customers singing his company's praises. He saw firsthand that people responded to authenticity, and realized it was the only way to go.

As companies move up the levels of the maturity, they see results. Those wins spur them on to try more, as they work their way up ever higher. They discover, either by accident or through careful strategy, that advocate marketing is the right way to grow a company.

To illustrate further, the opposite of this mindset is when companies try to achieve savings by cutting corners with their customers. When you last stayed at a hotel, for example, do you recall a small card inside the room declaring that the housekeepers will only collect laundry if specifically indicated, to save water and electricity and "help the environment"? On the surface, this sounds altruistic, but doesn't a tiny part of you grumble that the hotel is also saving big bucks by cutting that corner? It comes off as disingenuous, and in an effort to shave dollars from the bottom line, that hotel has lost your trust in its authenticity.

Level 5 companies achieve industry dominance because they've built a continuous positive feedback cycle. They have built their business processes around a systematic and actionable customer experience loop.

BUILD A COMMUNITY AMONG YOUR CUSTOMERS

"Increase opportunities and incentives for discussions about the one thing that they all have in common: your product or service."
—BRITTNEY COLLIER, MARKETING COMMUNICATIONS SPECIALIST, BILLTRUST

"Provide them with opportunities to engage with one another, virtually, in person, or on the phone."
—CHRISTINE MOREE, SENIOR ADVOCACY MANAGER, BMC SOFTWARE

"Building an entire ecosystem around the customer is not a one-step process. But the rewards your company can reap, together with the community you build and the personalized service you offer, are an investment that will pay dividends for years to come."
—NICK CHAMBERS, PRODUCT MARKETING, CLINICIENT

"I think the biggest community-building activity we have had with our members thus far is the moderated discussions forum inside Influitive. Our members have truly taken to it without much push from us. They see the value and are incredibly motivated to help each other; it's inspiring!"
—EMILY ELY, MEMBER MARKETING SPECIALIST, WEBPT

Behind the Scenes of Advocate Marketing

As a practice, advocate marketing is new and different; it involves motivating human beings as *individuals*, not as the targets of slick ad campaigns. Being curious is an excellent attribute for the advocate marketer. They must constantly be listening for what is said and unsaid. They engage, but as a good friend, not a nagging acquaintance.

They have the ability to find, engage, and nurture relationships with customers who are willing to actively participate in a variety of opportunities.

One of the first questions many of Deena's clients ask her is how many customers they should invite into their new programs, and where those advocates can be found. The answer depends on the strategy and goals of the program. In some cases, an invite-them-all approach is appropriate; other times, a selective, phased launch is more fitting. It all starts with knowing who your potential advocates are in the first place. This can certainly be a pain point, especially with nine out of ten companies telling us they don't fully trust their data. So, how do you know *who*, and *how many*, to invite?

The end goal is to get to a place where *everyone* is invited. However, if your customer communities are not yet well-nurtured, it may be necessary to start off with more of a selected process.

Most organizations already have some form of customer marketing program. More often than not, there are many customer programs in flight, although in a loosely associated kind of way. Whether it's a customer support portal, a learning management system, a community board, or a social media account, customer touch points are typically already well-established and plentiful. It's within these existing programs that you will find your first wave of advocates: *the friendlies.*

These known advocates are the ones you should pull into the conversation early and often. Ask them what they would want to see in a new advocacy program in terms of member benefits and opportunities. Take the time to interview a small number of them; take the time to understand their experience to date and build a plan that aims to enhance that experience. Understand through the friendlies what you will need to do to nurture the average customer along to full-fledged, card-carrying advocate.

Engaging your friendlies first is a tried-and-true approach. It's a way of connecting legacy customer programs to the brave new world of advocacy. It's a way to recognize the valuable contributions of those already actively engaged customers as you prepare to extend your reach beyond them. Asking your known advocates to help shape the first iteration of your program is not only a great way to build affinity, it's an excellent strategy to build an advocate-first program.

Failing to include your friendlies in the conversation as soon as possible may even have an adverse effect. Those customers who have been with you from the start may feel cold-shouldered, should you miss the mark with them as you build your program to launch.

Your known advocate group is also fertile ground for finding net-new advocates—those customers who aren't anywhere on your radar, but who are eager to get on board with your new program via word of mouth. Advocates of a feather flock together.

Once your friendlies are engaged, it's time to look further afield. This is where data becomes your best ally.

DEEP DATA FISHING

The total number of potential advocates you invite into a program is correlated to how much advocacy you intend to drive. As such, if you have massive targets to hit, you'll require a certain volume of active advocates. Working with more modest targets? You'll need to scale the membership accordingly. In either case, to get a close approximation of how many customers will join your program, you will need to work backward using your own email marketing data.

Inviting Your Advocates

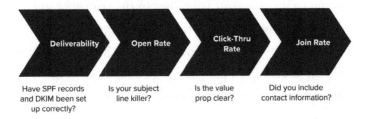

Here's an exercise you can do right now. You'll need your email marketing database or application open in front of you.

Find an email marketing asset that has a close link in terms of potential advocate audience. Typical assets of this type include:

- Invitations to customer events
- Customer newsletters
- NPS or CSat mailers

You are looking for an emailed asset from which you can derive the typical open rate and click-through rate (CTR) for your intended audience. You'll need these two data points in a moment. Feeling eager? Pull the open rate and CTR for a few assets, and get your averages in hand.

Using your actual open rate and CTR, begin playing with potential invitation numbers using the following formula:

1,000 invites × Open Rate × CTR = Total number of potential joins

You will need to take this equation one step further by taking into account that not all the people who land on your application or sign-up page will actually join, and not all who do join will actually engage. A rough estimate to use is 60 percent. Add the multiplier of 0.6 to your equation:

1,000 invites × Open Rate × CTR × 0.6 = Total number of joins

Once you have the total number of invites and joins roughly estimated, it's time to go fishing in the murky depths of your CRM. If you are lucky enough to have hundreds of thousands of customers, you may need to narrow the field; if you are a smaller shop, you may consider a come-one-come-all approach. If you do need to narrow the field, base your selection criteria on your program goals and objectives. Select those customers who have the attributes that will help you drive against those goals, whether that is based on location or title or product use tenure. At the very least, you could aim for customers who have provided a favorable NPS or CSat score in the past twelve months.

If your company, like many organizations, has questionable open and click-through rates, you may need to consider one of the following options:

Inviting many thousands of customers and hoping for the best.

Enhancing the invitation process beyond the invitation email. This could include any number of add-ons, including a phone call; a mail-out of a small, yet unique gift ahead of launch; a video invitation; or a handwritten invitation. Whatever it is, make the invitation spectacular and memorable.

STRATEGIC RECRUITMENT

More important than asking how many people to invite is aligning your recruitment and promotion strategy to your program goals. The *who* and the *how many* should tie directly into the results you are looking to achieve. You may even find through this exercise that your program goals are not realistic, given your total customer base or your ability to reach them. Setting your organization's expectations and developing your recruitment scheme accordingly from the outset will help you knock it out of the ballpark.

DISCOVER

Creation of a new advocacy program involves a process of a discovery. As a business, you're discovering what advocacy is, why it's meaningful, who your potential advocates are, and what will motivate them. In the discovery phase, it's simple to dig into customer databases and build lists of potential fits for the program. It's also easy to use a Net Promoter Score or satisfaction surveys to find advocates.

There may be active members of existing communities, or even entire support communities that already exist and are related to your business. Anyone offering help and answering questions in these groups will be a good fit for an advocacy program, as will active social media users, particularly on your own social media channels. Peek in on all the nooks and crannies to locate potential fits.

Who are you going to invite aboard? What's going to motivate them? What will the program look and feel like? What's the tone? What's the wrapper you're going to put it in?

Social media is an oft-overlooked source of potential advocates. The value of a large Twitter following is obvious, but pay attention to the quality of followers in terms of sphere of influence. Know who's tweeting at you and whether their sentiments are positive or negative.

It's natural to be overly cautious in the discovery phase, but it isn't necessary. The worst that can happen with someone you invite to join is that they don't. There's no risk in asking. There's a huge risk, however, in failing to go wide enough and souring a relationship with someone who feels they've been a super-advocate all along, and now feels left out.

The discovery phase relies on an invitation program. If your front-line operators, such as service and sales representatives, have positive interactions with delighted customers but have nowhere to send them, that's a problem. If all they can provide is a survey, an opportunity to recruit advocates is lost.

As such, provide incentives for your service and sales staff, like small rewards for those who do a great job finding and inviting advocates into the program. Someone, somewhere in your company, knows where the advocates are. That person may not be in your marketing department, so make it easy for everyone in your organization to invite quality advocates in; make sure the recruitment process is well known throughout the company.

Sales and advocacy can overlap in other ways, too. One advocacy program at SMART, for instance, carried a great deal of prestige as an invite-only membership. Salespeople used the program as a carrot in their sales process, offering to invite ten teachers at the signing school into our advocacy program. That wasn't part of the official program, but it worked.

It's simple to find advocates among a small number of customers. For a business with millions of customers, on the other hand, identifying advocates is problematic. Large companies often track their social media marketing with tools like Hootsuite, or a Salesforce tool called Radian6. A single click in these applications can identify who's tweeting or Facebooking about you, and invite them to your advocate program. The potential advocate receives a message saying, "Hey, thanks so much for the shout-out. I appreciate it. You deserve credit for these things you are doing for us. We want to do more for you, so we'd like to invite you into our program."

Integration tools make the discovery process more efficient, but they won't do the work for you. Take a systematized approach and move methodically through your invite process with each and every potential advocate.

So far, we've talked about ways the company can find advocates, but there are also ways for advocates to find you. Landing pages with a click-through form can serve this purpose well. For a SaaS product, there can be a message about the product itself, like a purchase screen that pops up when someone first uses the product. Events work the same way: if you have a presence at a large industry event, potential advocates will approach you to self-identify as fans. They want to tell you they love what you're doing. Close the loop and invite those fans into your program right away.

NURTURE

Nurturing is what you do to invest in the relationship after an advocate has joined your program. This is the phase when you take time to learn about them, as they learn more about you and the program. The most important aspect of the nurturing phase is listening. Understand who your advocates are. That means paying attention to their behaviors in the program and your interactions. Be advocate-focused.

While the relationship is mutually beneficial overall, at this stage, *you're* putting your best foot forward to make the advocate feel at home. Think of your new advocates as familiar friends rather than formal visitors: they should be made to feel that they can put their feet on the coffee table and raid the fridge when they're hungry.

Establishing this level of relationship demands investment. It *can* be financial, but it's always a relationship investment as opposed to a transactional investment. Nurturing requires more than a quid pro quo, like a gift card in exchange for a review. Cashing in at this phase leaves both parties unsatisfied, dissolving any chance at a long-term commitment.

Interactions that encourage a comfortable sense of belonging don't have to be complicated. They can be small, like reaching out and thanking someone for stopping by. Tell them it was nice to see them and start a conversation. Authentic interactions shift the program from the corporate mold into a more personal realm. They promote the crucial sense of authenticity.

Make it clear to your advocates that your company's staff are real people, just like them. You may be a corporation, which is a *legally fictitious* person, but you aren't an anonymous, automated entity. On the contrary, you are a group of people with the same fears, desires, and needs as everyone else.

When reaching out to advocates, be aware of what is happening in their lives. Listen in on social media to find out what's important to them prior to contact. Did they just get a promotion? Did their son or daughter just get married? Find a point of connection before launching into deeper conversation to further the relationship. Five minutes of research on an advocate pays a high dividend of loyalty and commitment.

It's tempting to skip or fast-forward through the nurturing phase because it's less measurable. The best advocacy, however, is built on a solid relational foundation. Don't skimp on this part of the equation; you'll get more out of your program if you invest in nurturing at the front end. It's hard to quantify, and you'll probably spend more money than you'll immediately see in return. That's exactly what an investment is.

Nurturing advocates means looking carefully at their needs and goals. MuleSoft, for example, focuses on developer advocacy, which can be a challenge, because many developers are naturally introverted. Mike Stowe, Head of Developer Advocacy at MuleSoft, helps them network. He might identify an interesting topic to feature on the company's blog, and invite an expert to write about it. If the developer writes up a blog post, Mike's team will polish it into something the person can use to accelerate their career.

Helping advocates grow their careers is one form of social capital that they earn with their efforts. Bestow awards on them ad help them produce things they value. The most effective advocates are involved in a variety of activities: they lecture, write content, connect people, and close deals, among other things. The more they do, the more loyalty they feel.

One of the most rewarding parts of advocacy programs is the fact these relationships grow over time. You'll learn more about them, their likes and dislikes, and how to best reward them. Ideally, the relationship is strong enough that your advocates will be open and honest with you about the things that would motivate them to participate.

MOBILIZE

Mobilization is where the money is in advocate marketing. The end goal of investing time, energy, and emotions to nurture advocates is to *mobilize* them.

Mobilizing means asking your advocates to do things on behalf of the company. Common mobilizations revolve around the Three Rs of Mobilization:

1. Referrals
2. Reviews
3. References

The full value of advocacy goes far beyond the Three Rs, and we don't generally recommend focusing on these metrics until your community is well-nurtured. However, when you're ready to focus on them, the Three Rs are the low-hanging fruits of advocacy. They're easy to quantify; there's a visible straight line from referrals to deal closure. The impact on revenue is clear. As companies mature in their understanding and execution of advocacy, though, they broaden their horizons. They start to consider relationship value and its impact on KPIs.

Marketo reached a 92-percent retention rate with its advocacy program. When they first set out, retention wasn't even on their radar as a key objective of their program; like many others, they focused on referrals, reviews, and overall engagement or relationship development. The retention piece of the puzzle, which is highly valuable and easily measurable in dollars and cents, was an additional positive benefit.

Companies mobilize their advocates in a variety of ways. Advocates are good at spreading your message in social venues, writing white papers to amplify your company as a thought leader in a particular space, or breaking through the chatter at industry events by virtue of their numbers and their passion, turning up the volume around your presence at conferences and trade shows. Activity of this kind only happens after advocates have been discovered and nurtured.

Mobilization is the dividend of investment. The relationship has vested, and you can now ask for favors that will be enthusiastically performed.

There's a key distinction between simple mobilization and advocate mobilization that is worth noting here. An email from an online review company asking for a product review in return for a $10 Starbucks gift card is mobilization, but it isn't advocacy. Simple mobilization is pay-for-play, a short-term strategy.

Better, stronger, more fruitful programs are much more relational. The best ones elicit strong, measurable, and meaningful advocacy with little required incentive because the *program* is the incentive. Companies that allocate dedicated resources to advocate marketing demonstrate their commitment to the success of their programs.

THE CAMPAIGNS-BASED APPROACH: PLANNING FOR SUCCESS

The long-term success of an advocate marketing program requires a certain alignment of stars. You need a whip-smart advocate marketer who can build out a scalable program on a solid foundation of business goals and objectives, and is willing to check their progress against targets frequently and fearlessly. You need the right platform to connect with your advocates and integrate with your CRM, among other systems. And you need to find your happiest customers who are ready, willing, and able to actively participate.

From the outset, most of this is straightforward marketing work. Hire the right person for the role, get the right tools, and dredge your database for folks who meet certain criteria, like 9s and 10s on a recent NPS or top contributors in your existing support community. However, advocate marketing isn't a just-add-water type of practice. Generating a frenzy of activity at launch isn't a stretch, if you know your audience and have invested time in crafting compelling, perfect-match opportunities and activities, incentives, and rewards. But then what? What happens when the new-program-smell fades? Well, that's the hard part.

Seeing advocate engagement dip a month or so after a brilliant, successful program launch typically causes concern, which is quickly followed by a mishmash of quick-hit activities and ill-fated advocate perks and communications: "Come back! Get a $5 gift card!" "Was it something we said?" "Tell us why you don't like us anymore!" These short-game tactics don't tend to offer much in the way of long-term gain—blatant incentives, impassioned pleas—neither lend themselves to genuine customer advocacy. Instead, this type of transactional approach stands to erode the value of your program for both you and your advocates. As a last-ditch attempt? Sure, why not. Throw it against the wall and see if it sticks. What if there were a smarter way to design your program right from the get-go?

TIMING IT RIGHT

Mobilizing advocates around your core metrics doesn't happen organically. Hitting your numbers requires a highly strategic approach that focuses on the overall advocate experience by delivering a steady stream of curated content and opportunities to the right advocates at the right time. We call this the *campaigns-based approach*.

In Influitive terms, a campaign is defined as a coordinated series of challenges with a theme or focus that is designed to achieve one or more core success metrics for the customer. These packaged sets of highly engaging experiences and challenges help keep an advocate program fresh and appealing to advocates as new campaigns are rolled out on a regular cadence—monthly, for example. This approach solves for a lingering issue prevalent with all types of marketing: time. The amount of time an advocate can dedicate to participating in program-related activities can vary greatly from one week to the next. It is not realistic to expect community members to spend several hours of every week in your program, contributing to your business for the long term. Instead, your goal is to prime and ready advocates to actively participate at very specific times with a focus on specific outcomes.

Calendar campaigns—delivering sets of themed content designed with a specific metric in mind on a predictable basis—allows your advocates to plan their time with you at the moments that matter most to your business and your program goals. Common themes include holidays, back-to-school, and sporting events.

ADVOCATES IN THE SALES FUNNEL

Invite advocates to events like sales demos and road shows. Ask them to speak with new prospects and provide recommendations or referrals. Tying advocacy to sales increases buy-in from the sales team, which probably already has a short list of customers when they need references, testimonials, or case studies. Those customers do burn out, however. An advocate marketing program provides an easy and effective way to identify, organize, and mobilize customers best suited to each of these requests from a larger pool of advocates. Then your sales team can help pick the advocates most relevant to their prospects' industry, seniority, and use cases.

Engaged advocates are happy to refer friends to your brand. Whether you post a referral challenge, run a referral contest, or actively ask for referrals, your sales team will be thankful if you score them more high-quality sales leads.

Advocates are valuable at all stages of the funnel. Here's how that looks in the sales process:

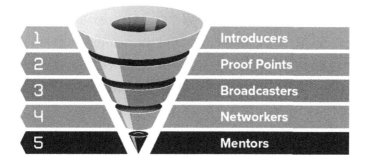

1. INTRODUCERS

Cold-calling has its place, but is more effective if someone else is picking up that phone for you. Find introducers and ask them for referrals. Allow contacts to take an active part of building a pipeline. More than 42 percent of Influitive's 2015 revenue was the result of referrals.

2. PROOF POINTS

Talk to customers and learn their stories. Get permission to retell them, focusing on the individual and your personal connection. Publicly publish the stories with pictures of your proof point throughout. Personal stories feel more authentic to buyers.

3. BROADCASTERS

Your prospective buyer isn't interested in talking only to you, nor do they care to learn about your company from your website. Encourage happy customers to talk about you everywhere else on the web. Buyers are more persuaded by comments on pages you don't own: review websites, social media, LinkedIn groups, and community forums, among others.

4. NETWORKERS

Reference calls may be a common part of the sales process, but they're often done at the wrong point in the buyer's journey. First, position reference calls as an opportunity for favorite customers to build their professional relationships. Next, connect them to buyers early in the sales process, and let them develop a relationship that doesn't feel transactional. Finally, find ways to thank, reward, and recognize your references, and they'll be glad to step up whenever needed.

5. MENTORS

Your customers' ability to contribute to your success doesn't end at the point of sale. Find your most passionate customers and let them take new customers under their wing. Don't wait to notice a customer is struggling before stepping in.

As reliance on peer validation in the buying process increases, reps can expect sales leadership to start asking about these roles in pipeline meetings. It's easy to lose an account on your own, so connect prospects with successful advocates willing to champion your product.

WHAT CAN YOU DO TODAY TO INTRODUCE ADVOCACY INTO YOUR SALES FUNNEL?

"Ensure Sales is well-versed on what we do in your customer advocacy program, so it's something they *want* to share with their customers, and not a 'chore.'"

—CHRISTINE MOREE, SENIOR ADVOCACY MANAGER, BMC SOFTWARE

"Explain how much more money a lifetime customer is than having to go out and find a new one. Discuss SaaS and how subscriptions make the consumer choosier."

—KAREN MOFFATT, GRAPHIC DESIGNER, GENOLOGICS, AN ILLUMINA COMPANY

"Present high incentives for referrals."

—BRITTNEY COLLIER, MARKETING COMMUNICATIONS SPECIALIST, BILLTRUST

The Evolution of
Advocate Marketing

Rob McEwen was in trouble. His junior gold mining company, Goldcorp, wasn't turning a profit. It had produced a disappointing 50,000 ounces of gold per year from its promising Red Lake property in Northern Ontario, and would be out of cash in a few quarters. Raising more money from the public markets would be difficult given the low productivity of the mine.

His geologists were stumped. Several data points showed that there was likely a lot of gold on the property, but after years of searching, the rich veins were still left untapped. Perhaps the gold was much deeper underground. But where? It would cost a fortune and more time than was available to drill the number of deep search holes required to find it—and it was not clear that his engineering team had the technical expertise to find the high-grade ore at depth.

With these problems on his mind, he attended the renowned Birthing of Giants conference for CEOs and entrepreneurs at MIT. It was mid-1999, the time when the first open-source software companies challenged a then-dominant Microsoft in operating systems.

Linus Torvalds, the creator of Linux, took the stage and explained how he organized legions of volunteer software developers around the world to build a better operating system. The Linux project was a grassroots movement that felt like an exclusive tribe with a valuable mission to the volunteer developers. They could see the impact of their work on the project every day, and they earned social capital in the global developer community. Many of these developers worked harder on the Linux project on nights and weekends than they worked at their day jobs.

In Torvalds' solution, Rob saw potential to solve his own problems. He had huge amounts of data on Red Lake, but did not have the time, money, or expertise to find what he was looking for. What if he could recruit the world's armchair geologists to engage on the project?

Over the protests of his technical staff, Rob made available to the public all of the data he had on Red Lake. Then he announced a $450,000 prize for anyone who could locate the main vein of high-grade ore. The prize inspired thousands of virtual prospectors, and not just geologists—mathematicians, experts in 3-D visualization, data scientists, graduate students, military engineers, and even non-technical people submitted proposals.

Like the Linux developers, people from different realms of expertise began to work together to find the gold online, like a giant international treasure hunt. One collaboration between a geologic consulting firm and a leading-edge computer graphics company created a powerful 3D map of the property. The map showed the Goldcorp team where to drill.

They found over $6 billion worth of gold deposits over 110 sites. That's at 2000–2001 prices—in 2017 terms, it's more like $24 billion. More than half of those sites were completely unknown to the Goldcorp geologists. The contest also cut the exploration time by several years. Goldcorp is now the second-largest gold mining company in the world, and the most profitable. These amazing results are all a result of Rob McEwen open-sourcing his proprietary mining data and mobilizing the world's virtual prospectors to effectively do what his own team could not.

The story of Red Lake's treasure shows us the future of how effective companies will operate. The division between employee and other stakeholders like customers, partners, platform developers, investors, and enthusiastic industry participants will be far less clear, and in some cases will vanish completely. After all, the world's largest transportation company, Uber, owns no cars, nor directly employs drivers. The world's largest accommodation company, Airbnb, owns no hotels, and does not employ lodging staff. The world's most robust encyclopedia, Wikipedia, has a tiny staff, and is maintained with an army of volunteers. The critical skill for success in this era of the social web is in building a system to discover, nurture, and mobilize communities of stakeholders. In other words, it is in building *relationships*.

Torvalds and the open-source movement has shown that, if organized properly, a global community of software developers can produce higher-quality software more efficiently. The advocate marketing pioneers featured in this book have shown that leveraging community is a better way to go to market as well. In fact, there is little that an employee can do that a properly organized and motivated member of the community could not do better.

What we see for the future is this: communities of enthusiasts become so infused into companies that it becomes standard operating procedure to leverage them in every part of the business, as routine as engaging employees to accomplish a goal.

MARKETING AND BEYOND

Advocate marketing has the potential to transform a business far beyond the marketing department, into sales, customer success, product development—teams that bring tremendous value to an advocate marketing program. The more diverse the internal champion and stakeholder set, the more appealing the program to advocates. The technical-minded advocate, for example, relishes catching software bugs, being first to solve support questions in your community, having access to information and opportunities that align with your product team, and building their own professional brand. You might attract such an advocate with exclusive membership benefits, as well as offers to speak at an industry event or build a relationship with your PR team.

Just as a cross-departmental advocate experience will grow a program because it's more targeted to the motivations of the individual advocate, the teams contributing from across the organization also benefit. The developer now has quick, easy access to beta testers and end users to run his ideas past; the media relations manager can source same-day quotes; the salesperson has a new pool of happy, referenceable customers who are ready, willing, and able to share their story with prospects. The more diverse and embedded advocate marketing is across a business, the higher the return on investment for both company and advocate.

Below is a department-by-department look at how advocate marketing can positively impact each team.

EVENTS

If there's a single sweet spot for advocate marketing, it's events. Whether they are small face-to-face events like user groups, or massive industry events like the Marketing Nation Summit, advocates and events are the ideal mix of happy customers and a high-energy social setting.

The best advocate marketing plans for large events are rooted in the overall event plan, which is typically the responsibility of an event marketing manager and should be available upon request. Study the overall goals and objectives for the event and align your advocate marketing efforts to support the top-line goals.

Is there a share of voice (SOV) metric? Plan a Tweetup.

Are booth staff hoping to scan 2,000 badges? Incentivize advocates to drive traffic to the booth.

Are there on-site sales meetings planned? Determine which advocates in attendance would be best to have on call, should the opportunity arise for an in-person reference.

Always align your advocate marketing plan to the master event plan to ensure you're delivering the right value at the right time, and raising your success profile within the organization. With all the event metrics in mind, however, don't forget to make the plan engaging. Events are the perfect venue for a highly gamified advocate experience.

ADVOCACY IN ACTION: CISCO EMEAR

Cisco EMEAR (Europe, Middle East, Africa, and Russia) had a vision for their program. They're an example of being primed and ready to dive headfirst into the deep end of advocacy. They embrace the advocacy mindset internally.

A large part of Cisco's strategy is structured around events advocacy. When they launched their program earlier this year, it coincided with Cisco Live—their flagship event—an annual event with thousands of attendees. This year, the event was held in Berlin.

The launch of Cisco's advocacy marketing program was linked directly to Cisco Live so that they were telling a cohesive story to advocates. Anyone who had registered to attend Cisco Live was also invited into the program, so there was cohesion between an onsite experience *and* the virtual experience of the advocacy program. Marrying the virtual and in-person aspects of an advocacy program is key for events marketing. The most successful programs incorporate an offline aspect.

Relationships can, of course, be developed to a certain point online, but until you get on the phone, or see someone on a webinar or in person, your relationship will be suspended in that virtual space. As an advocate marketer, your mission is to look every single one of your advocates in the eyes at some point. With Cisco Live, they mapped out an exciting gamified experience in their advocacy program, so that folks in the advocacy program received a next-level experience.

Advocates entered a big, inflatable dome with an open top, and inside the dome was a huge wraparound television screen playing videos on a loop about advocacy, why it mattered to Cisco, and what the program was about.

It was white-glove, with staff circulating trays of champagne. Registered advocates were allowed into the VIP area. If you weren't yet an advocate, you could register for the program and then enter this exclusive area. Cisco did a great job of amplifying what they were doing around advocacy, making current advocates feel special with exclusive VIP gamification onsite, and recruiting new advocates onsite, as well, with their advocacy dome.

Cisco Live is a high-budget, high-profile, company-wide event. The advocacy team strategically put advocacy on the map at Cisco. They had a splashy presence, and anyone at Cisco who didn't know the full scope of the advocacy commitment inside the business certainly saw it at Cisco Live.

Advocacy should be used to complement existing event plans, so that all events have some sort of an event plan or an event marketing plan. By leveraging and engaging advocates aligned with that plan, you're helping the business meet their goals, and helping meet their objectives for that spend, which, again, is important for such events.

PRODUCT

A company is only as good as the product or service it delivers to its customers. The best way to ensure your product meets expectations is through constant market feedback. However, getting authentic product feedback from your customers can be like pulling teeth. Why rely on surveys, focus groups, and beta programs when a powerful advocate program can give you real-time feedback in a fraction of the time—from your ideal customers?

CUSTOMER SUCCESS

Most companies say customer experience is a priority, but their teams aren't prepared or coordinated enough to make that priority a reality. It starts with a strong alignment between customer success and advocate marketing.

> "Advocacy will be the future of marketing because it isn't about simply trying something new—it's about results. It's clear that allowing your customers to speak for you is what drives marketing, because prospects want to hear from people like them."
> —VALERIO BATTELLI, CUSTOMER MARKETING EXECUTIVE, CISCO

This partnership has the power to unlock the true potential of your customers: genuine advocacy that will help you grow your business faster, not just through up-sell and cross-sell revenue, but through second-order revenue generated by advocacy.

CS teams can use an advocate marketing program to educate and motivate customers to become more successful, which will turn them into even stronger advocates. Posting product tips, case studies, and other helpful content can show advocates how to get the most value from your product, and speed up the onboarding process. Asking advocates to share their success stories and product tricks through your program will make it easier for CS to find and communicate stories with your content and marketing teams.

EVOLUTION DEPARTMENT BY DEPARTMENT

In this book, we've explored the ways in which advocate marketing has established itself as the road to success for future-facing businesses. The field, however, is essentially in its youth. What will advocate marketing look like as an adolescent concept, or when fully mature? How will this evolution translate to each department within your organization?

SALES AND MARKETING

To enjoy the full distribution potential of advocates, the advocate marketing platforms of today need to enlarge to embrace much more casual participants than deeply engaged stakeholders like customers.

The power of using advocates in sales and marketing lies in reducing prospects' fear of making a decision; this is done through trust, authenticity, and transparency. We see these platforms evolving so that they become the virtual equivalent of an intimate customer dinner, where highly relevant customer advocates are seated next to potential buyers and perform the conversion work directly.

Anyone who is enthusiastic about the idea behind a company should be invited in to the community and be encouraged to participate. As one experienced chief marketing officer told us about how he instructs his team on purchasing new software, "Before you become a customer, you should first be a member." The community will be the main place to understand the experience of becoming a customer, not the company website, email nurturing, or live customer conference.

We see the trend continuing with advocates playing a deeper role in all areas of distribution strategy and tactics. In everything from developing new positioning and messaging, to the creation of ads and the delineation of new pricing and packaging, winning companies will figure out how to get their advocates involved at the outset, and how to make them work well with their in-house staff.

CUSTOMER SUCCESS

There is a rich tradition of users helping users on support boards, going back to the 1990s. Oftentimes the best way to solve a tactical problem is to find people online who have solved that problem, and post a solution. By applying game mechanics intelligently, some companies have dramatically cut their costs of technical support.

We see support use cases as a small fraction of the full

potential of this idea. The customer success movement is about companies taking full ownership over the value received by customers. This is much more impactful than how, for example, a piece of software is used tactically. In order to take maximum advantage of a technology, a company needs to staff its rollout and ongoing management properly, integrate it into its value chains, and have the right metrics for success. These are items that the advocate community can play an important role in achieving for other customers.

We can see the root of this approach in local user groups, where users of products meet to discuss how they can improve their performance using those products. For many of the technology companies we serve at Influitive, these meetings appear spontaneously, without the prodding of company management. In fact, even though we have a vibrant advocate community, local user groups were initially created outside of it until we figured out how to bring them in. The common element to the local user group is geography—they are local, so people can meet face to face for a high-quality, high-bandwidth information exchange experience.

We anticipate that there will be many more of these types of groups, that some academics call *phyles*, with more axes of classification than geography. Industry, use case, and situations can be much more relevant than where the company happens to be physically located. For example, at Influitive, our companies tend to cluster around the identity of the advocate: educators, human resources professionals, office managers, chief financial officers. A use case, such as the generation of referral leads in the case of our own software, is an area where birds of a feather may flock together. All of these phyles can be most efficiently and effectively organized within the advocate community.

Increasing sophistication in customer success processes and technology has enabled better forecasting of when a customer is not experiencing sufficient value and may *churn*, or cease renewal of their subscription. Today, this will trigger some sort of an alert, and an account manager might call up the customer to see how things are going. For a variety of reasons, those calls often go answered.

What if, instead, the person calling was someone who has a similar industry, use case, and situation, a peer who can show how to generate a lot more value from the service? We see this as the future of customer success, powered mostly by advocates who participate because they believe in the mission, enjoy seeing their impact and value the social capital inside and outside of the advocate community.

PRODUCT AND ENGINEERING

Rob McEwen found his gold with an army of armchair geologists and engineers. The open-source movement is powered mainly by volunteer software developers. Carl Pei's OnePlus Forums helped design the game changing OnePlus One smartphone. One of the best-selling new flavors of potato chips in Canada was sourced by a Frito-Lay advocate who came up with the idea for a poutine flavor. Smart companies are tapping into their communities of enthusiasts for ideation and development of products. This is a trend we predict will accelerate.

We talked earlier about CarbonBlack, which has created a number of different committees where advocates can participate in product development. For example, the Design Committee is limited to a couple of dozen participants, who meet with the chief technology officer and team of product managers, designers, and engineers to collaboratively work on the next generation of product features. This is a level deeper than what we have typically seen in the past, which is mainly around ideation.

The best companies are putting their advocates into the lab to work hand-in-hand with technical staff. Companies that do this will not only build better products, but have a chance to create something that changes the nature of competition through faster learning and iteration.

STRATEGY, OPERATIONS, AND FINANCE

Of all the functions of a company, strategy, operations, and finance are closest to its core. It can be difficult to imagine how these core functions may be better performed by the advocate community than employees—yet we are seeing precisely such innovation.

Today, Lego enjoys one of the most valuable and beloved brands in the world. Their entertainment empire extends from branded toys to mobile apps, from feature films grossing hundreds of millions of dollars to theme parks and retail locations all over the world. It's hard to imagine that this once-humble, near-bankrupt producer of plastic bricks could be mentioned in the same breath as Disney, yet it's an apt comparison today.

There are multiple virtual and real-life communities at Lego that open-source their strategy to determine the markets they should compete in, and how to compete in those markets. There is a site called Lego Ideas, where anybody can suggest new products, services, and business lines. Winning proposals provide an opportunity to work with Lego executives. The award-winning and profitable Architecture line of Lego bricks, which is targeted at adults and sells for more than twice the price of Lego for kids, was the brainchild of a Lego advocate who created Lego masterpieces for fun and convinced top management that there was a profitable segment in adults.

Lego's brilliant CEO, Jørgen Vig Knudstorp, appointed in 2003, receives a lot of credit for his genius strategy. He in turn credits his communities of advocates with its creation.

Opening the company strategy to customer advocates encouraged even more innovation by making the company more transparent and trustworthy. An innovation site in Japan, Cuusoo, not only sources ideas, but pays royalties to the customer-innovators for life. The revenue-sharing model forced openness about company financials that built an even greater sense of community with its innovators. Cuusoo drove some of Lego's greatest contributors to its financial success with joint licensing deals with brands from Disney, LucasFilm, and Minecraft, all suggested and voted on by members of Lego strategic innovation communities.

Can company operations be better performed by the community? In the future, we see this being an instinct or reflex. The first people to consult on solving operational problems will be the advocate community.

MANAGING COMMUNITY ENGAGEMENT

In the future, we foresee advocate engagement platforms

that sense the different affiliations of advocates and provide the ideal experience for them that cuts across lines. Social media feeds are increasingly adapting to participants depending on their situation, and they provide a useful metaphor that may work well for the disparate communities in which advocates participate. Hierarchies are valuable tools for managing highly complex initiatives like global enterprise-wide advocacy, but ultimately, success is about the advocate user experience, which can cut across that hierarchy in multiple directions.

We also envision more of the benefits of advocacy shared with the advocates themselves, through stock ownership organized by a Blockchain mechanism. After all, they drive a lot of value for the companies and products that they care about, and having ownership encourages a long-term, more strategic approach to advocacy, as opposed to simple quid quo pro. Would this ownership cause advocates to be less effective because their integrity is compromised?

The answer is likely no, especially if the incentives are modest enough. We also believe that mechanisms will evolve that rate the effectiveness and trustworthiness of advocates, as a form of *whuffie*—a virtual currency that correlates to contributions to society in author Cory Doctorow's *Down and Out in the Magic Kingdom*.

We already rate the accuracy of advocates in our own minds, so it feels natural that we will see those mechanisms extended. On sites like Quora, Stack Overflow, and Reddit, this social capital is already being tracked and managed.

Marshall McLuhan instructs us to take every medium to its logical extreme to predict what it will *flip into*, as radio flipped into television and television flipped into YouTube. If a much larger population in the world is advocating, the quality of those advocates become crucial to understand.

When a company has a corporate-wide initiative to build advocates and mobilize them, organizational design becomes important for success. Who should be responsible for the success of the overall initiative? How can it be ensured that the overall program is cohesive, yet responsive to the needs of all divisions, departments, and geographies?

The GE rollout of its Six Sigma Quality Initiative points the way for how to manage advocate marketing in the largest of companies. First, there should be someone accountable for overall advocate engagement across all divisions, stakeholder types, and geographies. This Chief Advocacy Officer, reporting to the CEO, ensures that the power of advocates is being implemented everywhere, and the company is achieving its advocacy goals, moving up the capability maturity model.

Just as in major enterprise rollouts like Six Sigma, the complexity can be mind-boggling. If there are sub-communities for geographic locations, divisions, and stakeholders, how best to handle, for example, the needs of Japanese partners for a startup division of a large company, if there are advocate communities for Japan, partners, and the division?

There are no easy answers here. Often, the solution has already been identified through other global enterprise initiatives and how they are managed. It's the job of the Chief Advocacy Officer to figure out the best approach.

Conclusion

ADVOCATE MARKETING: THE BRIDGE BETWEEN YOU AND THE FUTURE

———

Selam's memory of her recently dead mother is searing as she walks a treacherous miles-long path to a muddy stream before sunrise. The water is dark, contaminated with leeches and virulent bacteria. She fills her jerry can with this water; full, it weighs twenty-five pounds. She will carry it the entire way home. It's a trip that the thirteen-year-old Ethiopian girl takes every single day, bringing life, but also sickness, to her family and village. The trip means she has no time for school; the other young women in the village are similarly prevented from focusing on their education because of the crucial need to fetch water.

This soul-crushing state of affairs continues until trucks arrive in the village one day. The trucks carry drilling equipment, pipes, and engineers. They dig wells and provide clean water. They completely change the destiny of Selam, her family, and her village.

A thunderous round of applause emanated from an art gallery in New York as several hundred people in their tuxedos and ball gowns reacted to the story they had just witnessed. They didn't just passively watch Selam's story in a film; they walked her path right alongside her. They met her family, experienced the tragedy of her predicament, and felt the emotional high when Charity:Water's trucks and workers began digging the well.

They experienced the whole story in virtual reality. With headsets strapped to their faces, they could reach out and touch the environment in 3D. The full immersion in Selam's story and Charity:Water's aid efforts created the desired result: everyone in the room donated, $2.4M in all, a massive amount for such an event and much more than the charity had anticipated. Many who donated before to the same cause were so moved by the experience that they donated several multiples more, like one executive who increased his donation from $60,000 to $240,000.

According to the filmmaker from Charity:Water, Jamie

Pent, presenting the story in virtual reality made all the difference in this stunningly successful campaign. The video has now been seen over a million times at events and on social media.

"It's so hard to understand the water crisis when you just hear statistics, and it's about individuals who are going through this just because of where they live," Pent said. "Any one of us could have been born there, and we weren't. But we have the ability to help."

Charity:Water is probably the most innovative nonprofit in the world. They have innovated in almost every sphere: their business model, go-to-market strategy, product development strategy, operations and logistics. Led by the mercurial former nightlife promoter, Scott Harrison, they are the first and only advocate-first nonprofit that we have seen.

Founded in 2006, Charity:Water has raised over $260M to provide clean water to the poorest people on Earth. They were the first to create the "100% business model", where operational costs were covered by founding donors so that the mass public donors had 100% of their money funding water projects. In order to do this, they had to set new standards for transparency and trust—a major problem for the oft-distrusted charity sector. They were the first to focus on iconic design to better attract donors, employees, and volunteers. They were the first to introduce an online community, mobilizing advocates to tell their stories and recruit their peers. They were the first to use transmedia storytelling to better connect emotionally with their audience over multiple media types.

In the last year, Charity:Water was also the first charitable organization to launch its own Blockchain-based cryptocurrency, the Clean Water Coin. They are pioneers in using machine learning, both in the field with smart sensors learning about water quality, and in their marketing efforts. On the marketing front, they were the first charity to build its own conversational bot, Yeshi, who is based on a real Ethiopian girl with water-fetching responsibilities. By using Facebook Messenger's responsive technology, the "Walk with Yeshi" experience uses a bot to simulate what it's like to walk for approximately two and a half hours to find clean water. The experience is interactive; the end user is prompted to answer questions, respond to quizzes, and take pictures. Meanwhile, Yeshi sends the user GIFs, videos, audio recordings, images, and written messages detailing her experience walking to get water. The donations received after users have this immersive experience are significantly higher than usual.

In Charity:Water, we can see a glimpse of what the future

looks like for top-performing, advocate-first companies. Such companies are intensely focused on human stories of change, and transparently and intelligently apply technology to more effectively deliver their message to all stakeholders.

HOW FUTURE TECHNOLOGY WILL IMPACT ADVOCATE MARKETING

We live in exciting times, with innovation accelerating in multiple sectors, each new advancement feeding off the last. These technologies will have a significant impact on the capabilities that companies have to discover, nurture, and mobilize their advocates.

AUTOMATION AND INTEGRATION

Automation that is integrated into every aspect of our digital lives will have a profound impact on the advocate experience, which is central to advocate productivity. Technology already exists today to embed parts of advocate programs inside other applications, making missions, points, leaderboards, and other components of advocate programs available everywhere online. Advocate programs will increasingly be systems of record for all advocacy that happens electronically.

Automation and integration will provide a better advocate experience by providing a single interface to drive more advocacy in less time—for example a single review challenge that publishes to multiple review sites simultaneously. More varied and personalized forms of rewards will also be available that are automatically issued to the advocate without human intervention. We also envision more relevant social capital being accrued, by integrating advocacy success into social platforms. Companies will compete to attract potential customers who are known to be effective advocates, through better terms and substantial discounts.

Companies will also benefit greatly from automation and integration. Automation will put the advocate community at the core of every go-to-market process, from strategic messaging to sales development; the first instinct of marketers and seller will default to mobilizing the advocate community to help solve their problems.

MACHINE LEARNING

If Marshall McLuhan were alive today, he would likely recognize machine learning as the technology of automation taken to its logical extreme. It is a breakthrough technology that allows computer programs to learn without explicitly being programmed.

Machine learning is advancing at a breathtaking pace. Deep-learning algorithms are beating the best human players in games like Go, a game that has eluded other software algorithms that use brute force combinatorics. On the healthcare front, by analyzing millions of images of breast cancer cells, machines can now detect certain types of cancer before human radiologists can. Once beset by spam email, our inboxes are largely now free of these messages because of machine-learning algorithms.

Now that there are advocate marketing platforms with millions of advocates performing billions of acts of advocacy, there is enough data to train learning algorithms. As advocates engage with these systems, we can expect that their missions, challenges, and rewards will be better tailored to their interests. Program administrators will be wearing their Iron Man suits, as systems recommend experiences to create to drive business goals. Administrators will not only be driving more value directly for advocates and their companies, but also training learning systems, which in turn will drive even more automation.

MESSAGING AND CONVERSATIONAL INTERFACES

Messaging and conversational interfaces are not new. What has changed is that most of the internet users in the world are now using messaging apps such as Facebook Messenger,

WhatsApp, WeChat, Slack, and Kik. These systems have nearly 2 billion users, and in many cases, messaging is a person's primary interface to the world. These interfaces are becoming smarter and more powerful, integrated with other systems, and more convenient to access. We believe that they will make a major impact on advocate marketing.

Advocate networks already exist on messaging systems. In China, most online advocacy happens in messaging-oriented social network WeChat, where genuine advocates compete with paid influencers. Slack focuses on instant messaging for business users, but it's easy to create an external hub for advocates that takes advantage of the Slack application that already exists on their devices. We think that the user experience of the future combines the engaging nature of challenges and game mechanics, with the permanence and searchability of a topic-oriented discussion forum, and the pervasiveness and immediacy of messaging.

The other major trend that we see in this area is the rise of "bots", which are software programs that users interact with via conversation. With advances in machine learning, these bots are becoming nearly indistinguishable from human communication. We see bots being used to enhance the ability of advocate marketers to build deeper relationships with many more advocates. Bots will also automate more advocate marketer tasks, executing with a sentence that which would normally take several clicks to do.

EARLY STAGE MAJOR TECHNOLOGICAL INNOVATION

Advocate Marketing will be impacted by every major technological wave that is sweeping the world today. As we saw with Charity:Water, virtual reality is starting to affect charitable giving; VR stories of advocates succeeding with products should make a similar impact. The Blockchain is enabling secure microtransactions, an innovation that could lead to advocates having a piece of the action for the companies they are helping to build. An edition of this book in ten years could well be discussing the impact that brain-to-machine interfaces are making on advocate marketing—one of the most exciting new platforms that is just starting to see significant adoption today.

STEP INTO THE FUTURE

Advocate marketing, in its purest form, is about people: what makes them passionate, what makes them engaged, what makes them contribute, and what transforms their lives.

You have the opportunity to experience the same transformation in your business and career. By creating a people-focused mindset throughout every stratum of your organization, you can create an environment of growth, connection, and, most importantly, trust.

We have seen firsthand the immense and powerful shifts that happen not only for companies that invest in advocate programs, but for the advocates themselves. They discover new avenues of pursuit they had not ever considered; their lives take on new shape and purpose. The companies that enjoy the loyalty of these advocates are similarly transformed, not only in revenue, but in mission. For many companies, sometimes for the first time, their mission and their message are aligned through one conduit: the ideal messenger they find in their advocates.

There has never been a greater premium on authenticity. Surveys indicate, in a recurring consensus, that millennials have a much higher bar for authenticity than the baby boomer generation. People demand to see the real you; there's no hiding behind the CEO mask or the cleverly-worded advertisement. Customers, at the end of the day, *want* to trust the people and businesses in their lives.

Since earning the trust of your customers must be your primary objective, and your customers—and buyers worldwide—have shown time and time again that their trust is earned most rapidly through the word of mouth of people like them, why not lean in to this paradigm? Why not orient your marketing strategy toward proving your authenticity as a company? The happy customers you already have are your best tool for gaining new customers. With a systematized and strategic approach to capturing and propagating their existing high praise for your company, you can transform your company's growth. You can create a messenger that *is* your message.

Advocate marketing isn't simply another tool in your tool belt; it is the way your business will become its most successful, and the most prepared for the future it can possibly be.

There is no time like the present to invest in advocate marketing for your company, and developing the skills of discovering, nurturing, and mobilizing advocates to further your career. We look forward to joining you in a bright future together.

About the Authors

MARK ORGAN is the founder and CEO of Influitive, a provider of solutions to help companies discover, nurture, and mobilize their advocates. Mark has been an innovator in marketing processes and technology for more than seventeen years as the founding CEO of marketing automation pioneer Eloqua, and he is a go-to-market consultant for software-as-service companies in North America and Asia. With a background in neurosciences and a passion for applied psychology, Mark is a dynamic writer with a unique vision for a more human approach to marketing.

DEENA ZENYK is a Principal Strategic Consultant who, with more than 10 years' experience in advocate marketing, is a world-leading expert and pioneer in advocate marketing. Her guiding professional principle is to make leading-edge marketing philosophies and practices accessible and actionable for the everyday marketer.

Made in the USA
Coppell, TX
06 September 2020